"Embark on a colorful journey through time with our captivating coloring book! Rediscover the vibrancy of youth as you delve into past eras, reminiscing about iconic landmarks and immersing yourself in the tranquil art of therapeutic mandalas. Designed to stimulate the mind and soothe the soul, this book offers an enriching experience through history and fun facts that encourages relaxation, creativity, and a zest for life. Our coloring book promises to ignite your imagination and rejuvenate your spirit."

"Let's now start by remembering some of the most important historical moments and also monuments in history and some fun facts about them."

Signing of the Declaration of Independence of the United States.

John Hancock, the President of the Continental Congress, signed his name with such large letters that his signature became synonymous with signing one's name. This is why in American English, "put your John Hancock" means to sign your name.

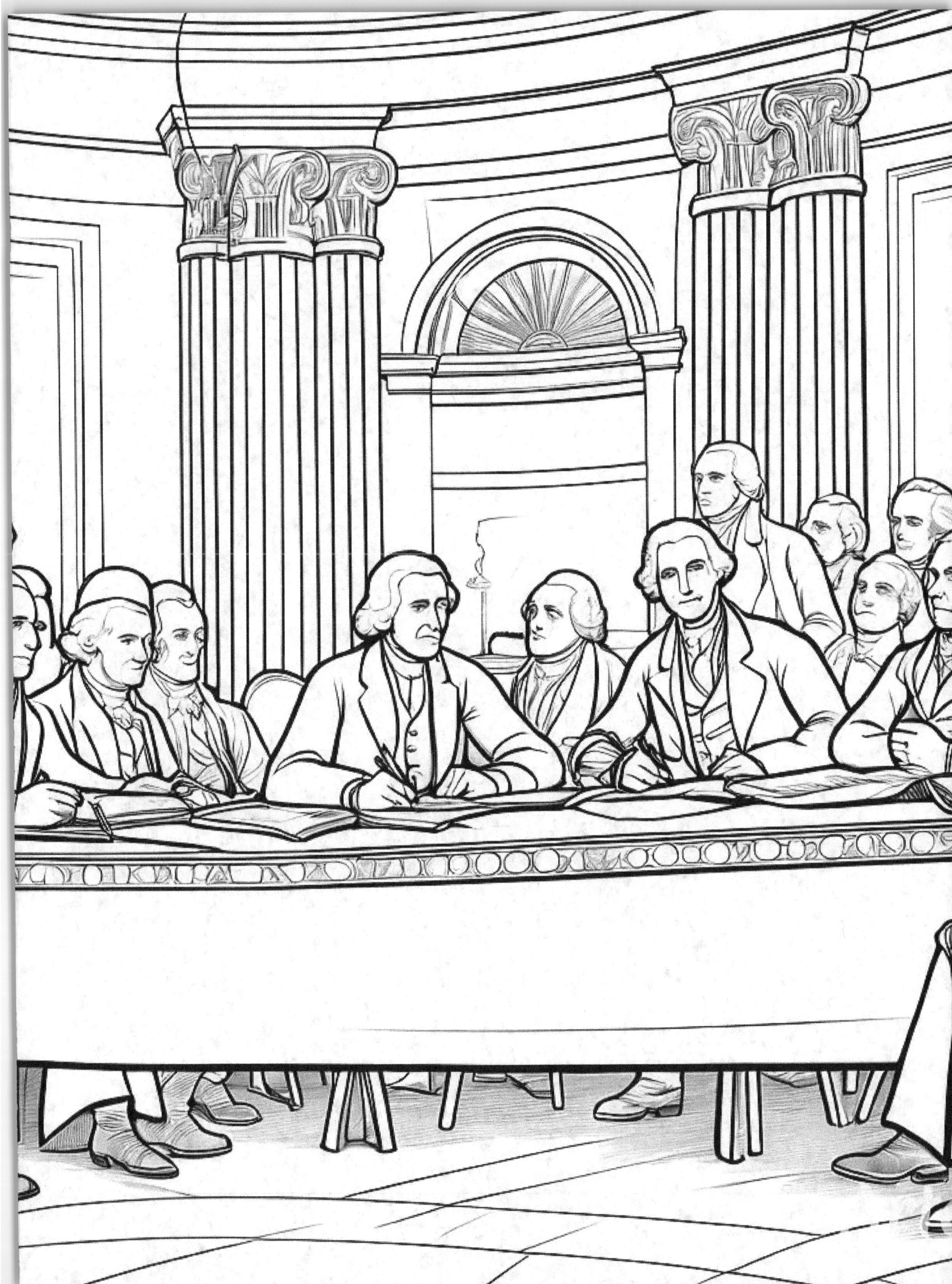

The Construction of the Pyramids of Egypt

Despite popular belief, the workers who built the pyramids were not slaves, but rather skilled laborers and artisans who were well-fed and compensated for their work. Additionally, evidence suggests that the workers were organized into teams and provided with medical care, showing a level of sophistication in labor management during that time.

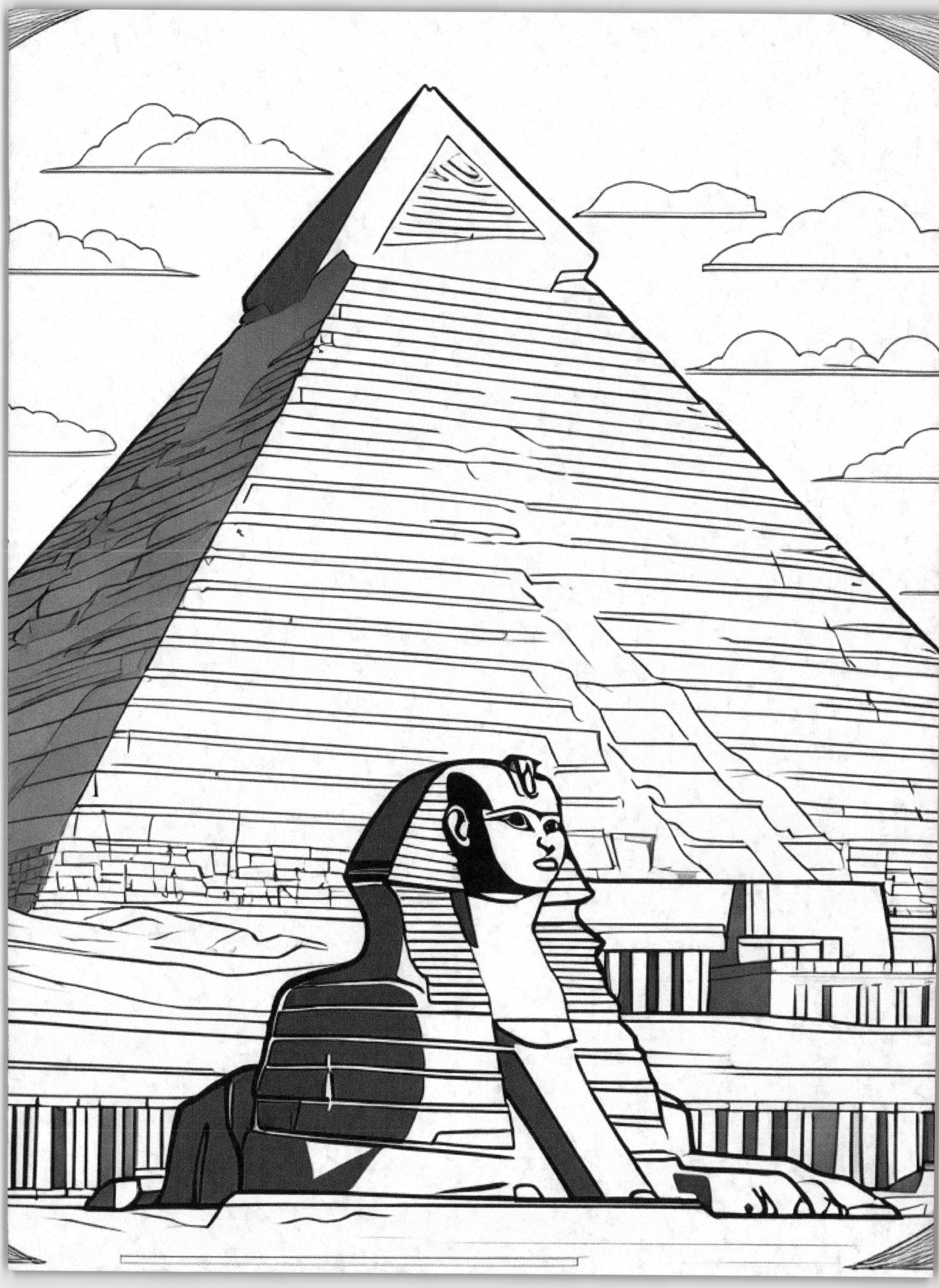

The Boom of the Automotive Industry in the 1950s

The Boom of the Automotive Industry in the 1950s led to the popularization of drive-in theaters across the United States. As more families owned cars, drive-in theaters became a popular entertainment option, allowing people to watch movies from the comfort of their own vehicles. This cultural phenomenon peaked in the 1950s and 1960s, with thousands of drive-in theaters operating across the country.

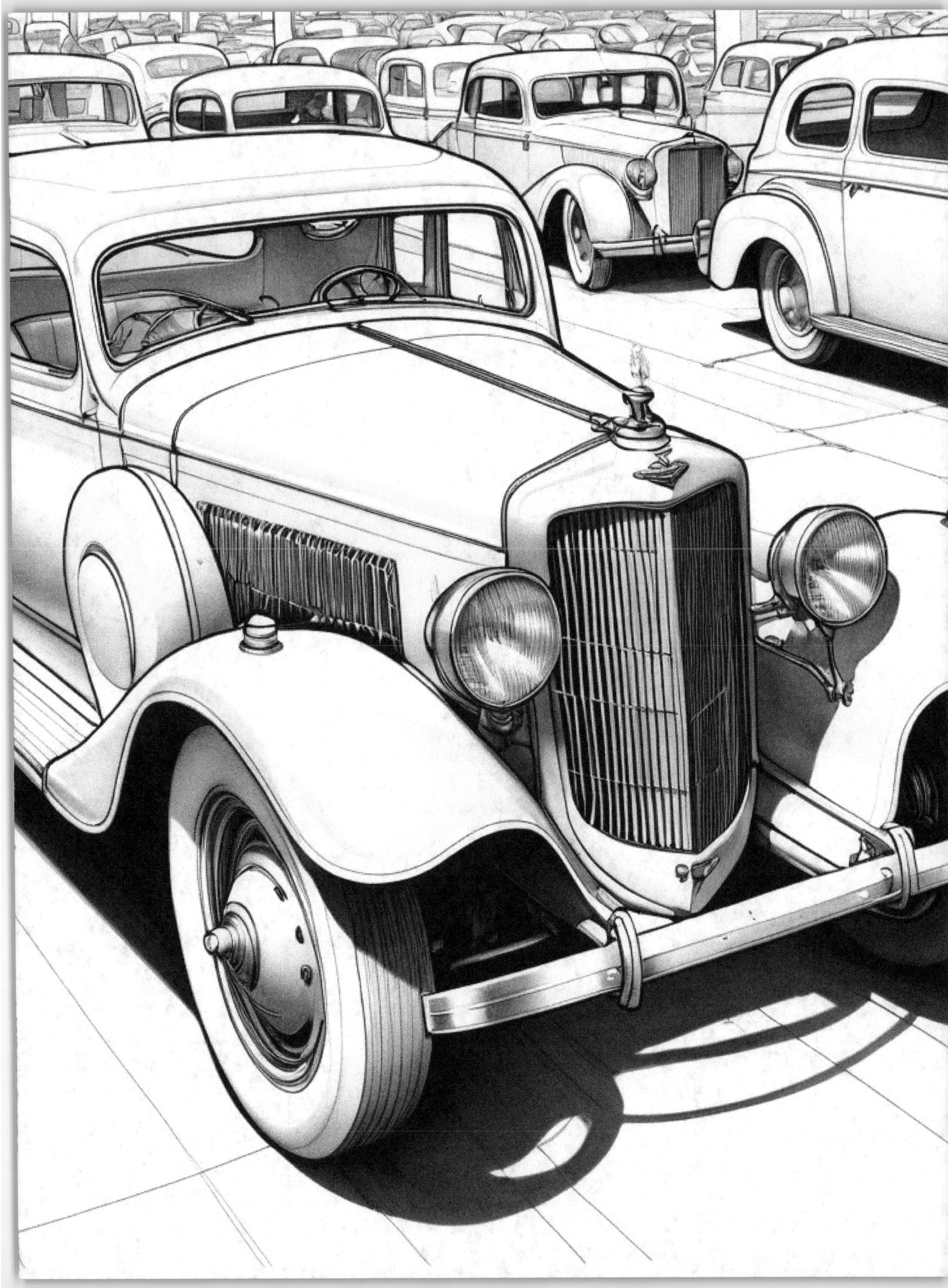

The Jazz Age and the Roaring Twenties

This Era saw the rise of illegal drinking establishments known as "speakeasies" during the Prohibition era. These hidden bars became popular venues for socializing, dancing, and enjoying jazz music while patrons secretly consumed alcoholic beverages. It was a time of rebellion against the prohibition laws, leading to a vibrant underground culture that defined the era.

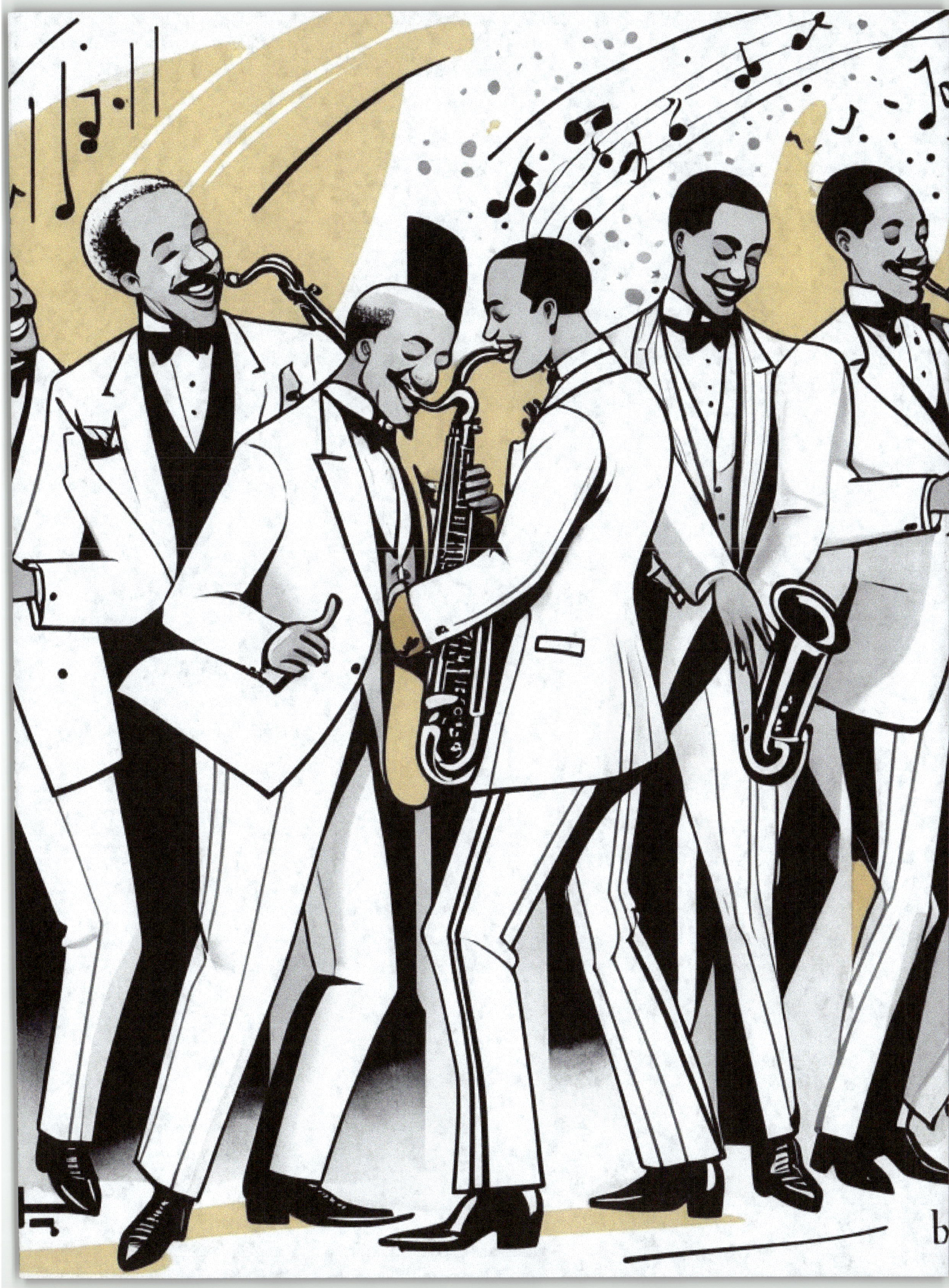

The Mysterious Terracotta Warriors in China

Each warrior in the army has unique facial features, hairstyles, and armor, indicating that they were individually crafted. Additionally, recent archaeological discoveries have revealed that the warriors were originally painted in bright colors, which have since faded over time. This adds to the intrigue and wonder surrounding these ancient sculptures.

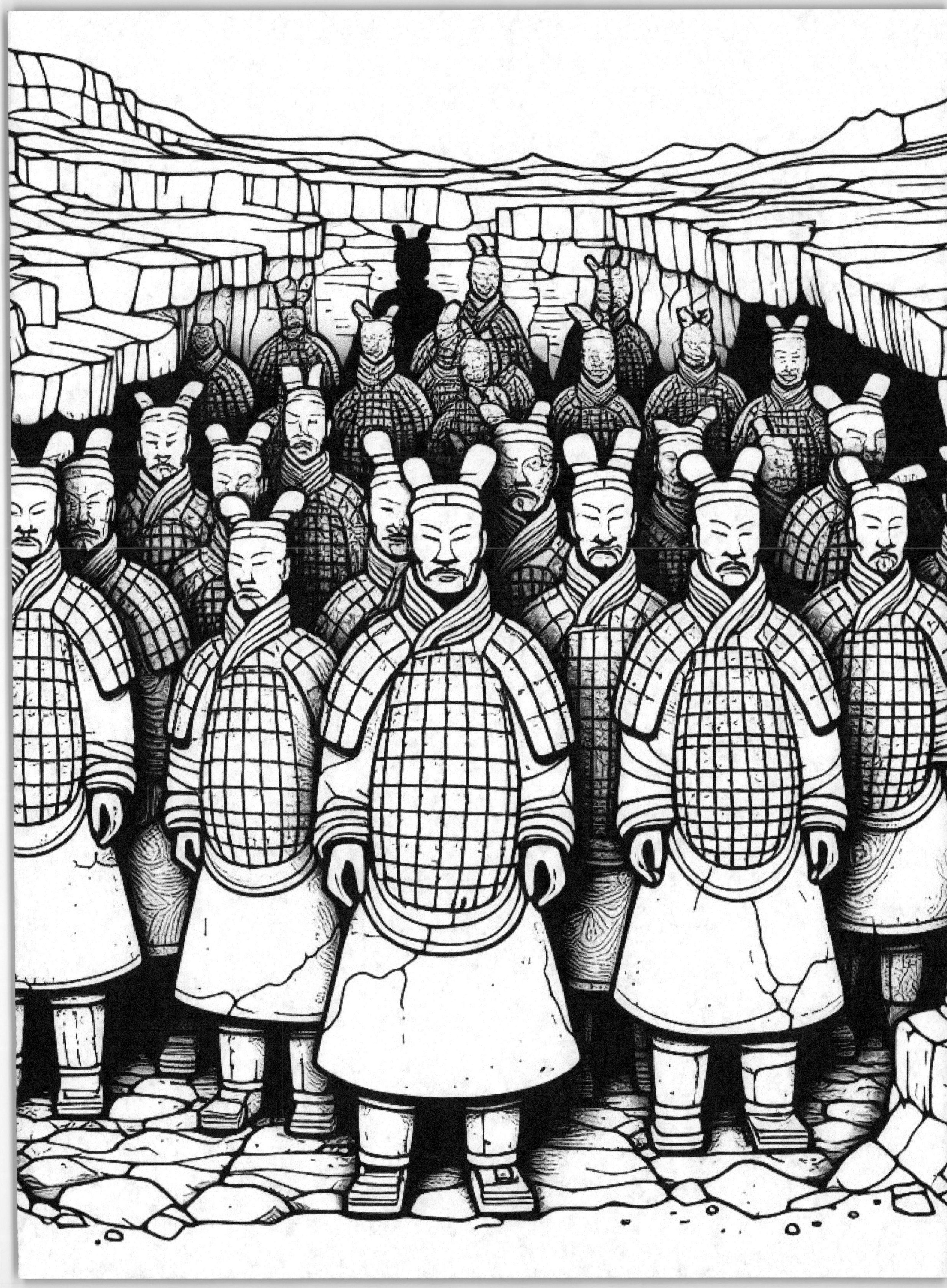

The Coronation of Queen Elizabeth II

This was the first coronation to be televised, allowing millions of people around the world to witness the historic event in real-time. The coronation took place on June 2, 1953, at Westminster Abbey in London, and the televised broadcast was watched by an estimated 27 million viewers in the United Kingdom alone. This marked a significant moment in the history of television broadcasting and royal events.

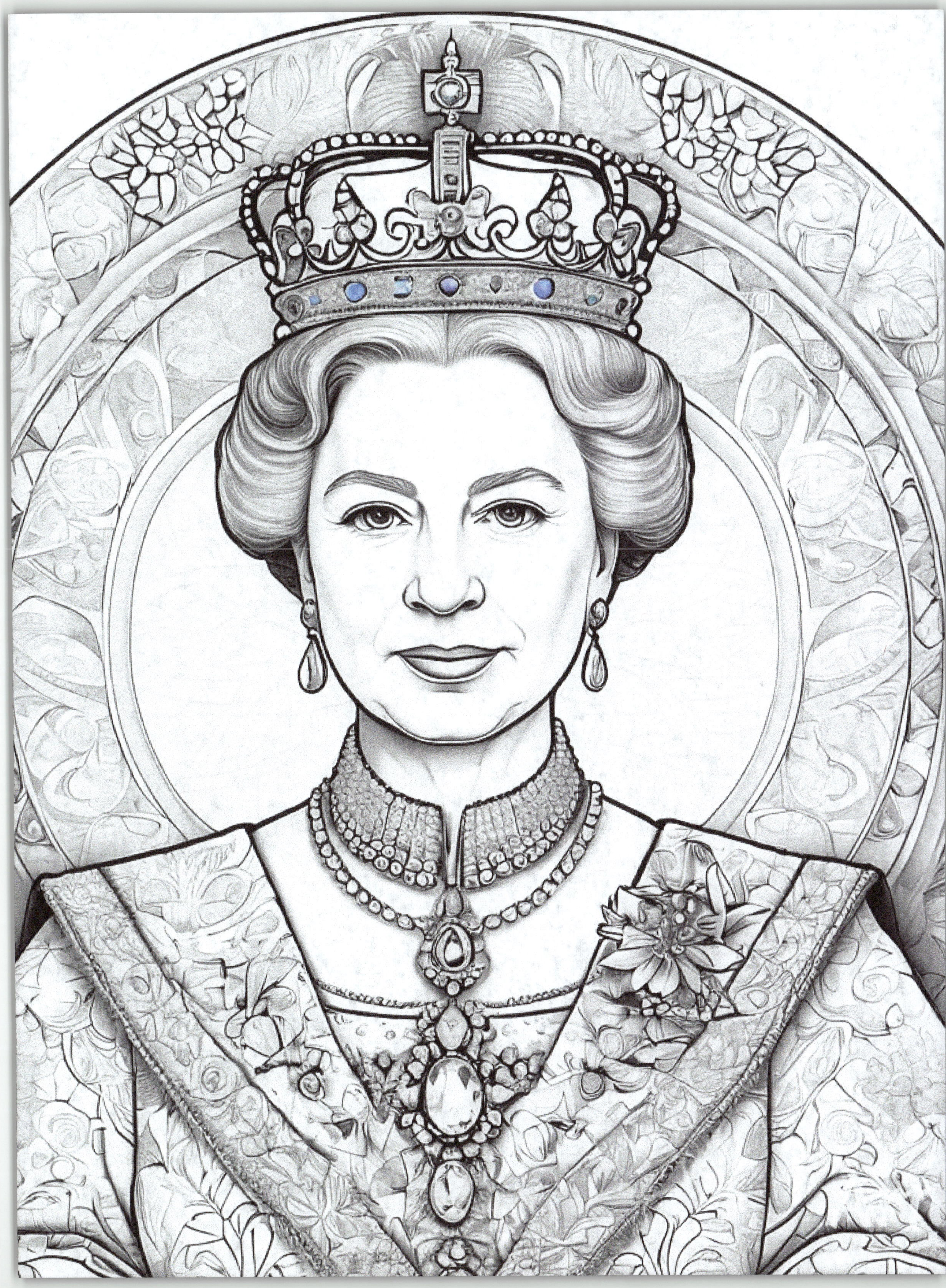

Now let's visit and remember some emblematic places.

Grand Canyon, Arizona

This is not only a stunning natural wonder but also home to a thriving ecosystem. Despite its arid appearance, the Grand Canyon supports a diverse array of plant and animal life, including over 1,500 plant species and nearly 500 animal species. From elusive mountain lions to iconic California condors, the canyon's rugged terrain provides a sanctuary for a wide range of creatures.

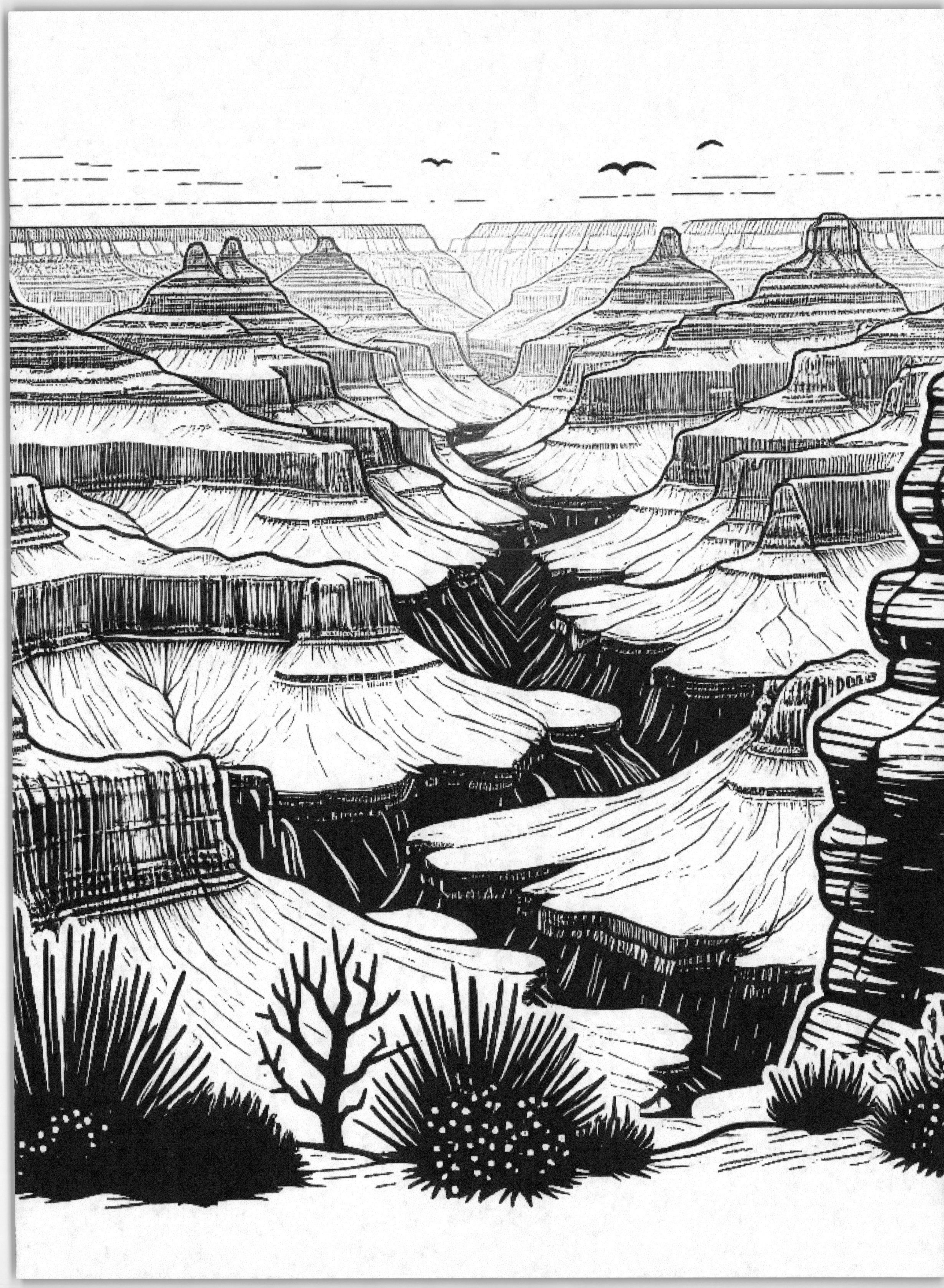

Yellowstone National Park

This is home of the largest concentration of geysers in the world, including the famous Old Faithful. Yellowstone's geothermal features are a result of the park's location over a hotspot of volcanic activity, creating a unique landscape of hot springs, mudpots, and fumaroles. Visitors to the park can witness these spectacular geysers erupting on a regular basis, providing a thrilling natural display of power and beauty.

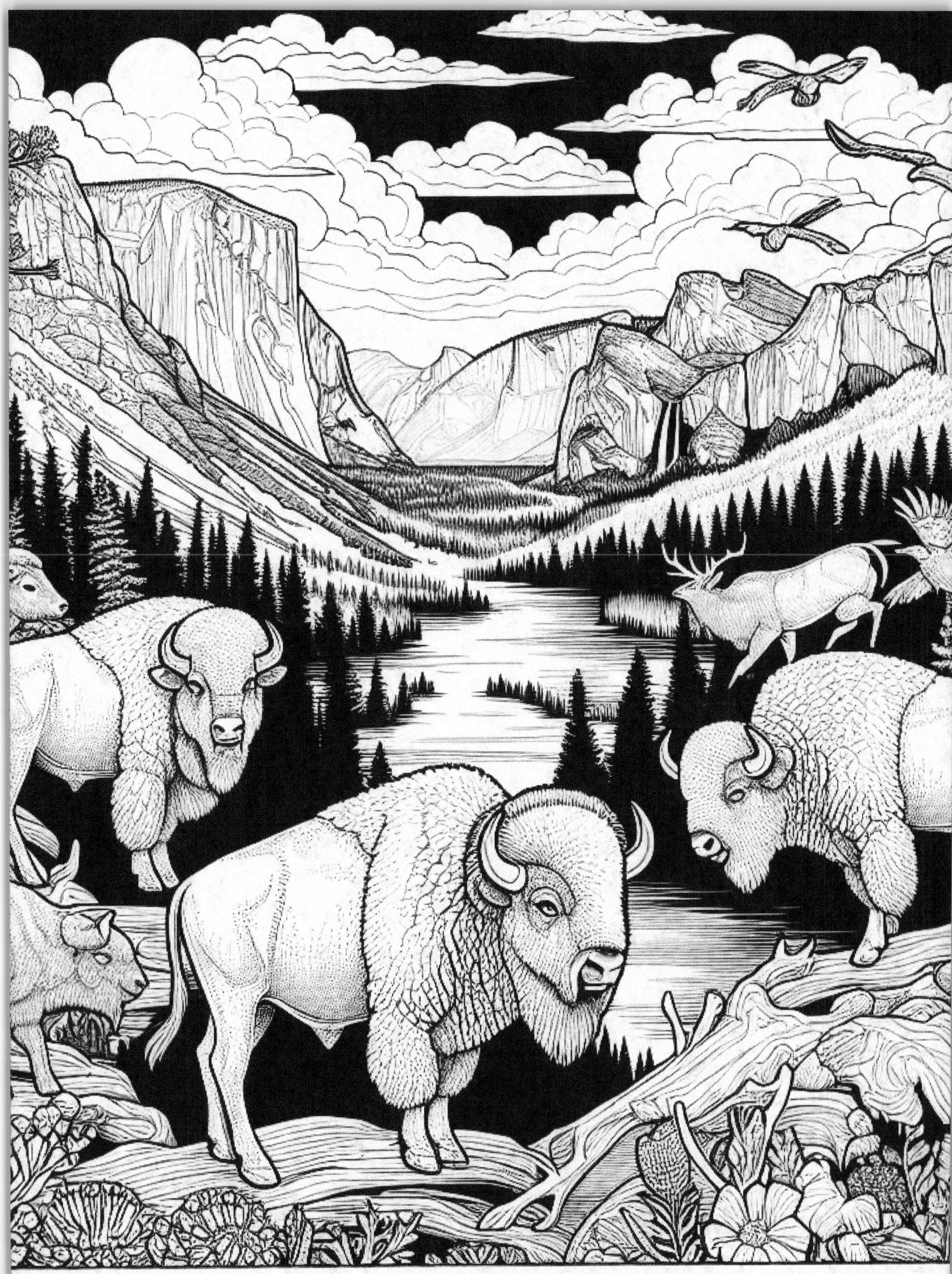

Machu Picchu, Peru

While it is widely believed to have been built as an estate for the Inca emperor Pachacuti in the 15th century, its remote location and lack of written records have led to various theories about its use, including as a royal retreat, a religious site, or even an astronomical observatory. Despite extensive research and excavation, the true purpose of Machu Picchu continues to intrigue and captivate visitors from around the world.

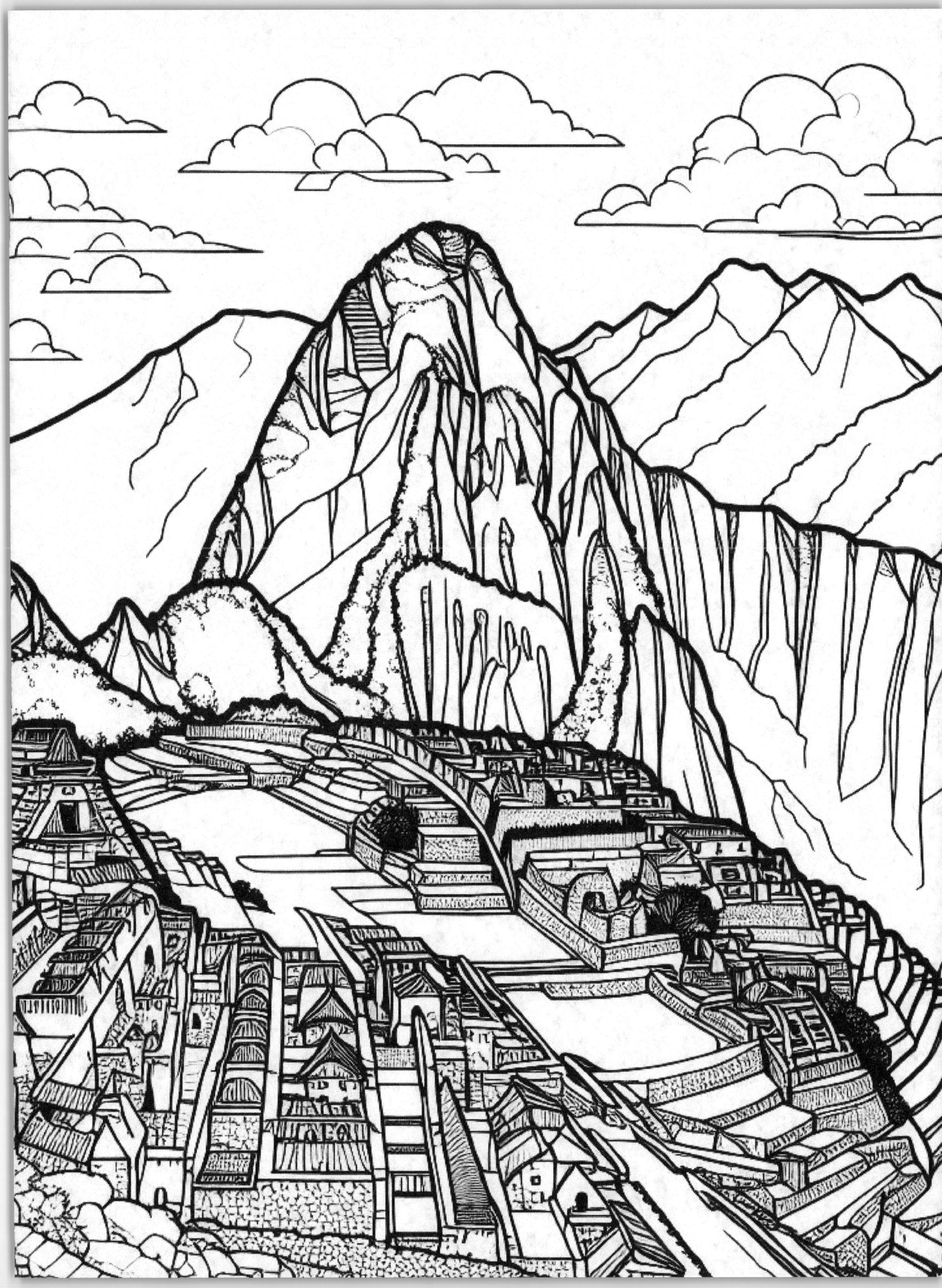

Acropolis of Athens, Greece

It served as the inspiration for the design of the United States Capitol building in Washington D.C. The architect of the Capitol, William Thornton, was inspired by the classical architecture of ancient Greece and specifically the Acropolis when designing the iconic dome and columns of the Capitol building. This connection between ancient Greece and the United States showcases the enduring influence of Greek culture and architecture on Western civilization.

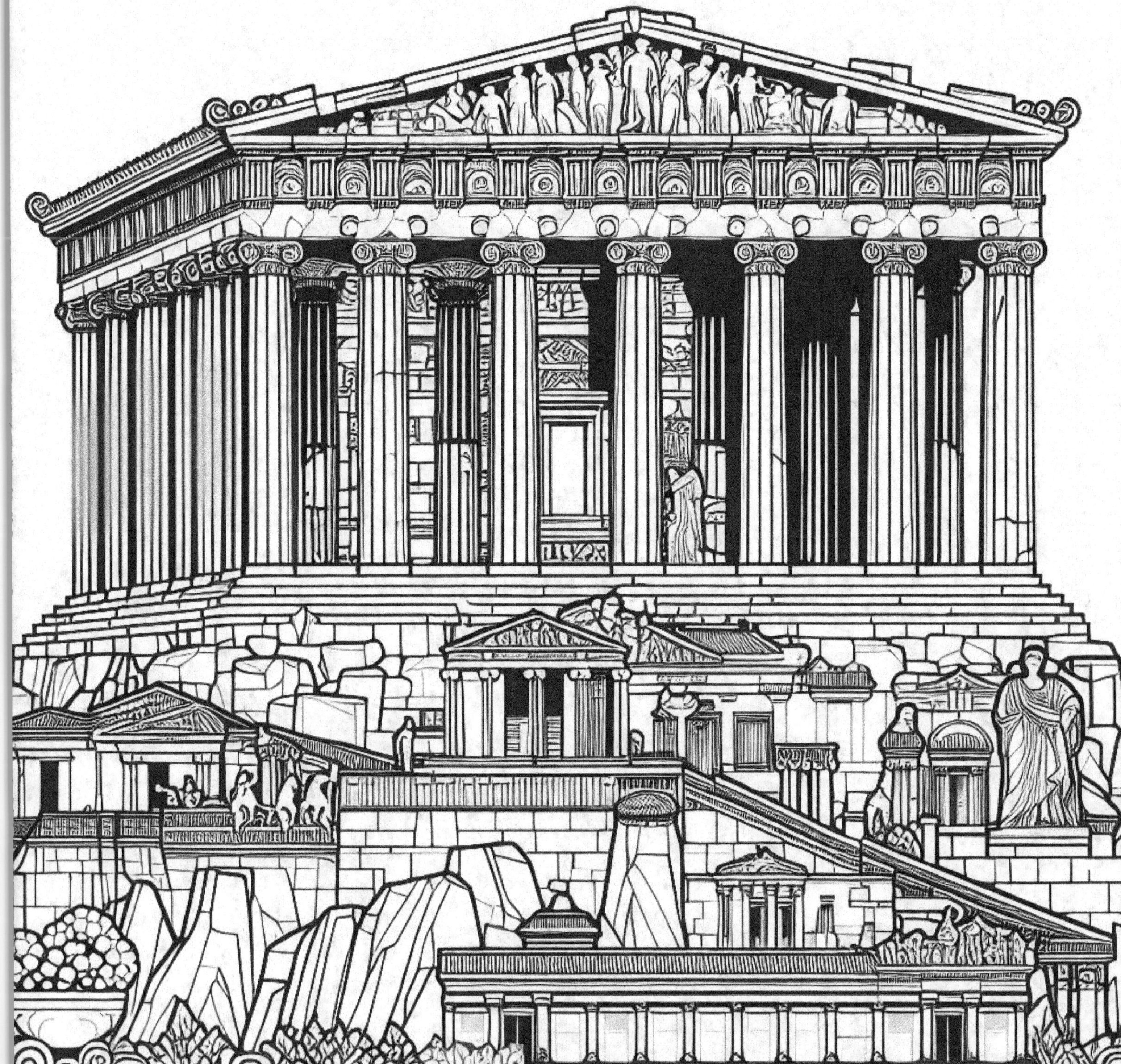

The Capitol, Washington D.C.

Its iconic dome is made of cast iron and was not part of the original design. The dome was added in the mid-19th century to symbolize the strength and unity of the United States. During the Civil War, the dome was left unfinished due to lack of resources, leading to the nickname "the great unfinished dome." After the war, construction resumed, and the dome was completed in 1863. Today, it remains one of the most recognizable symbols of American democracy.

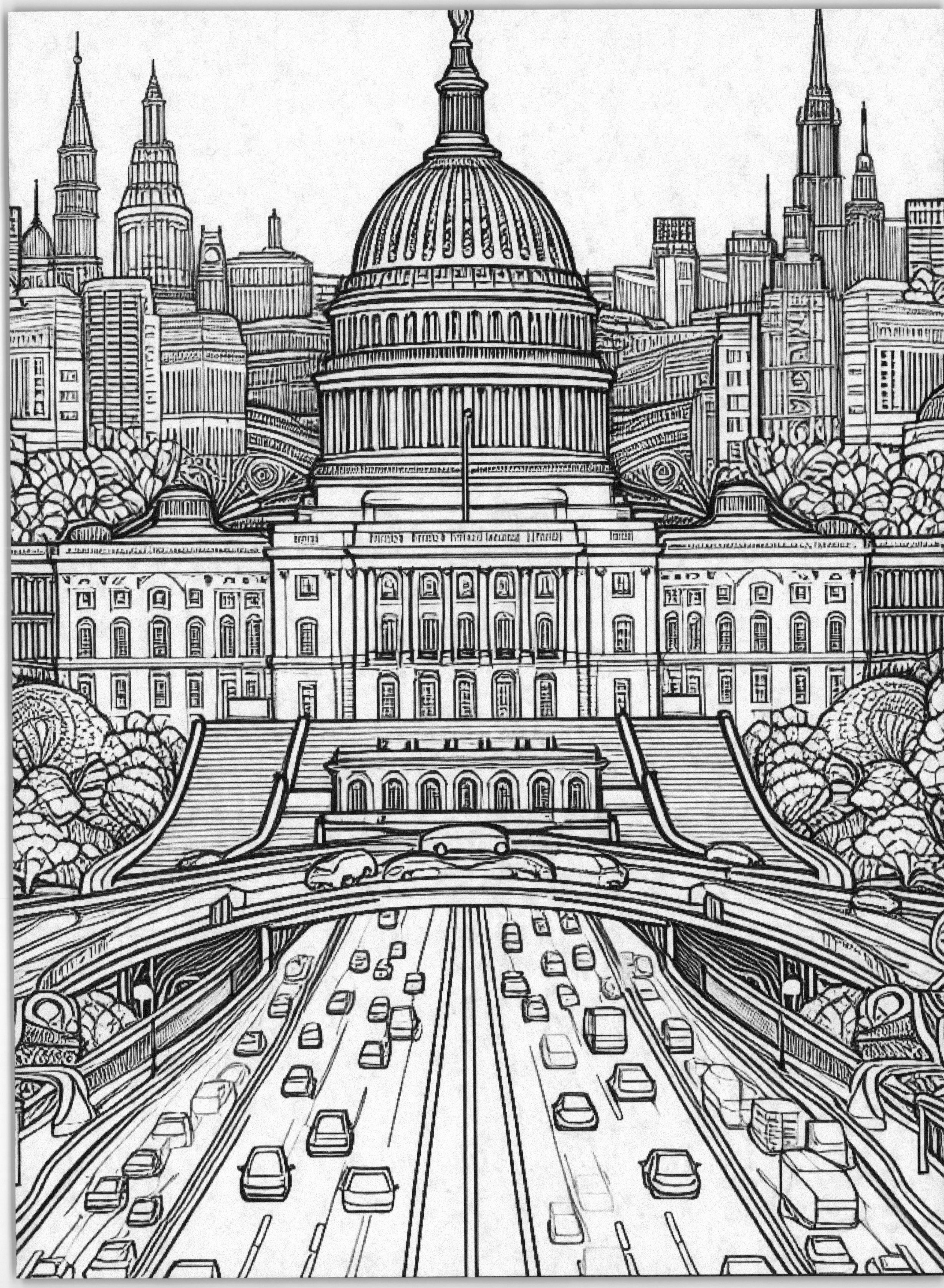

Roman Colosseum, Rome, Italy

It was the largest amphitheater ever built in the Roman Empire, capable of seating up to 80,000 spectators. Despite its size, the Colosseum was designed so ingeniously that the entire venue could be filled with or emptied of water within a matter of hours, allowing for spectacular naval battles known as "naumachiae" to take place. These mock sea battles were a favorite spectacle among the ancient Romans and showcased the engineering prowess of the time.

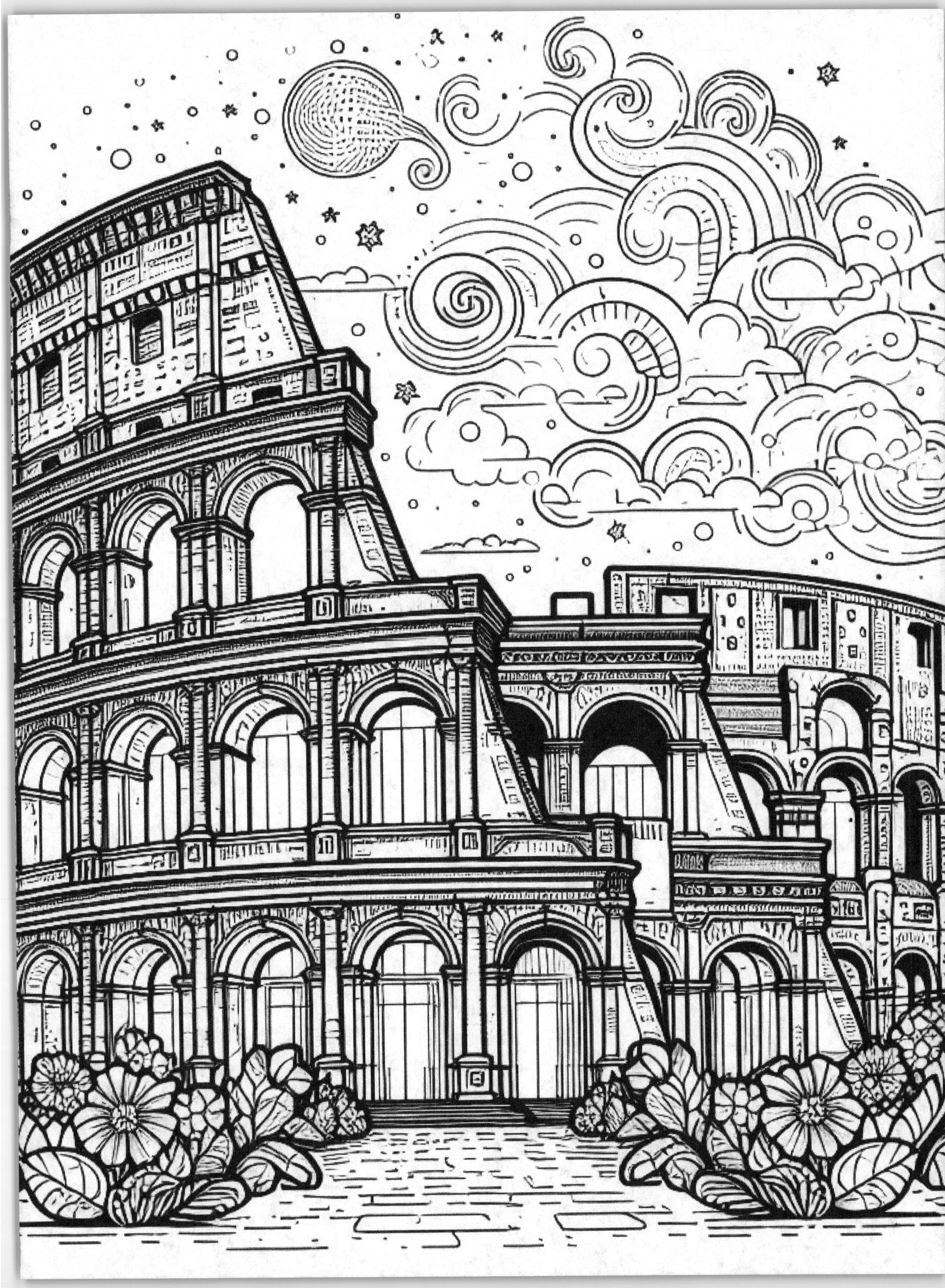

Great Wall of China

This is not a single continuous wall, but rather a series of interconnected walls and fortifications built over centuries by various Chinese dynasties. The construction of the wall began over 2,000 years ago, with different sections being built and rebuilt over time. Additionally, contrary to popular belief, the Great Wall cannot be seen from space with the naked eye, as it is relatively narrow compared to the vastness of outer space. However, it is still an impressive feat of ancient engineering and remains one of the most iconic landmarks in the world.

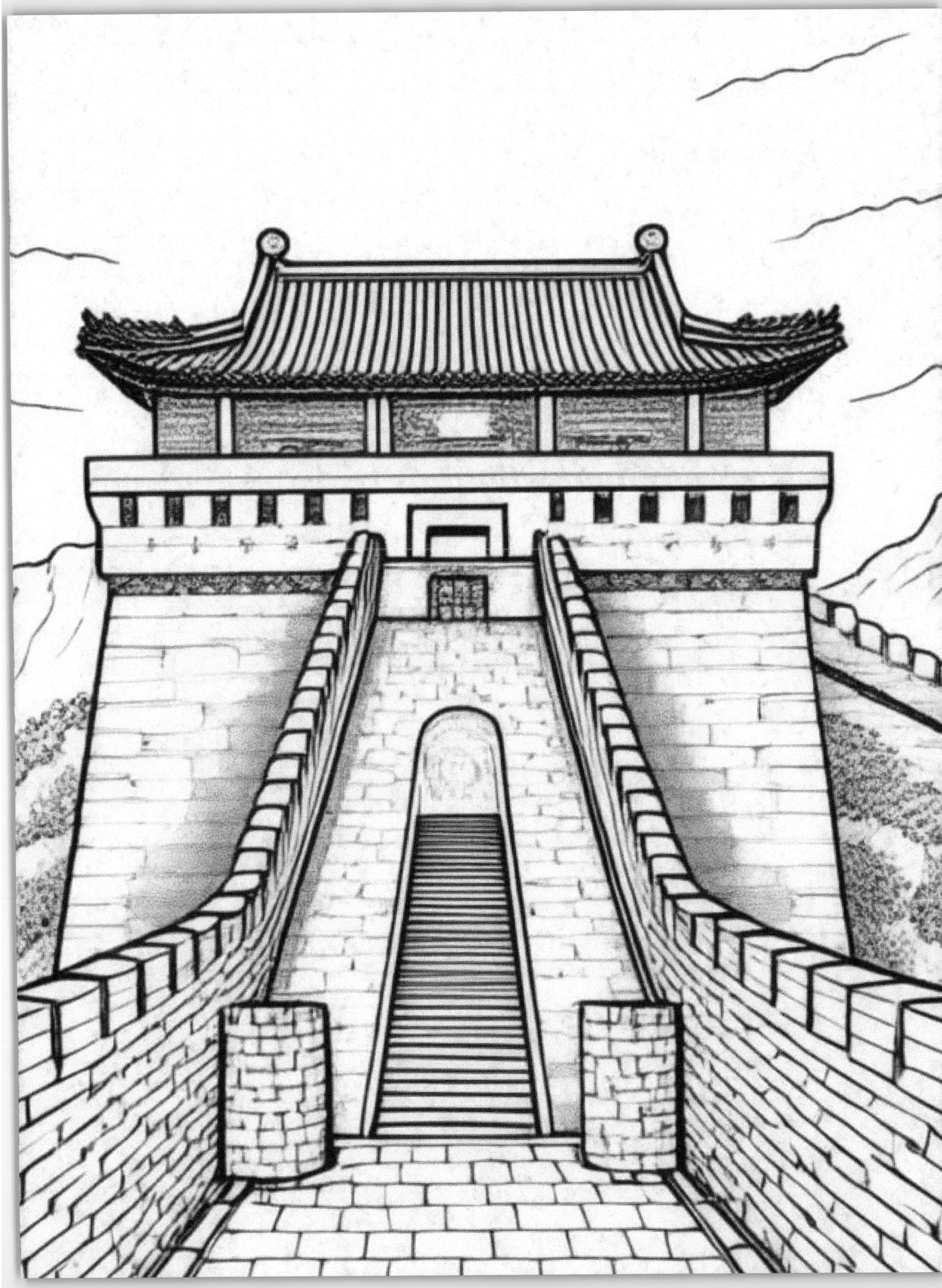

The Alamo, San Antonio, Texas

It was originally built as a Spanish mission in the 18th century, known as Mission San Antonio de Valero. The mission was established in 1718 and served as a home to missionaries and Native American converts. It wasn't until the early 19th century that the mission gained its iconic status as a fortress during the Texas Revolution. Today, the Alamo is a symbol of Texas independence and a popular tourist destination, attracting millions of visitors each year.

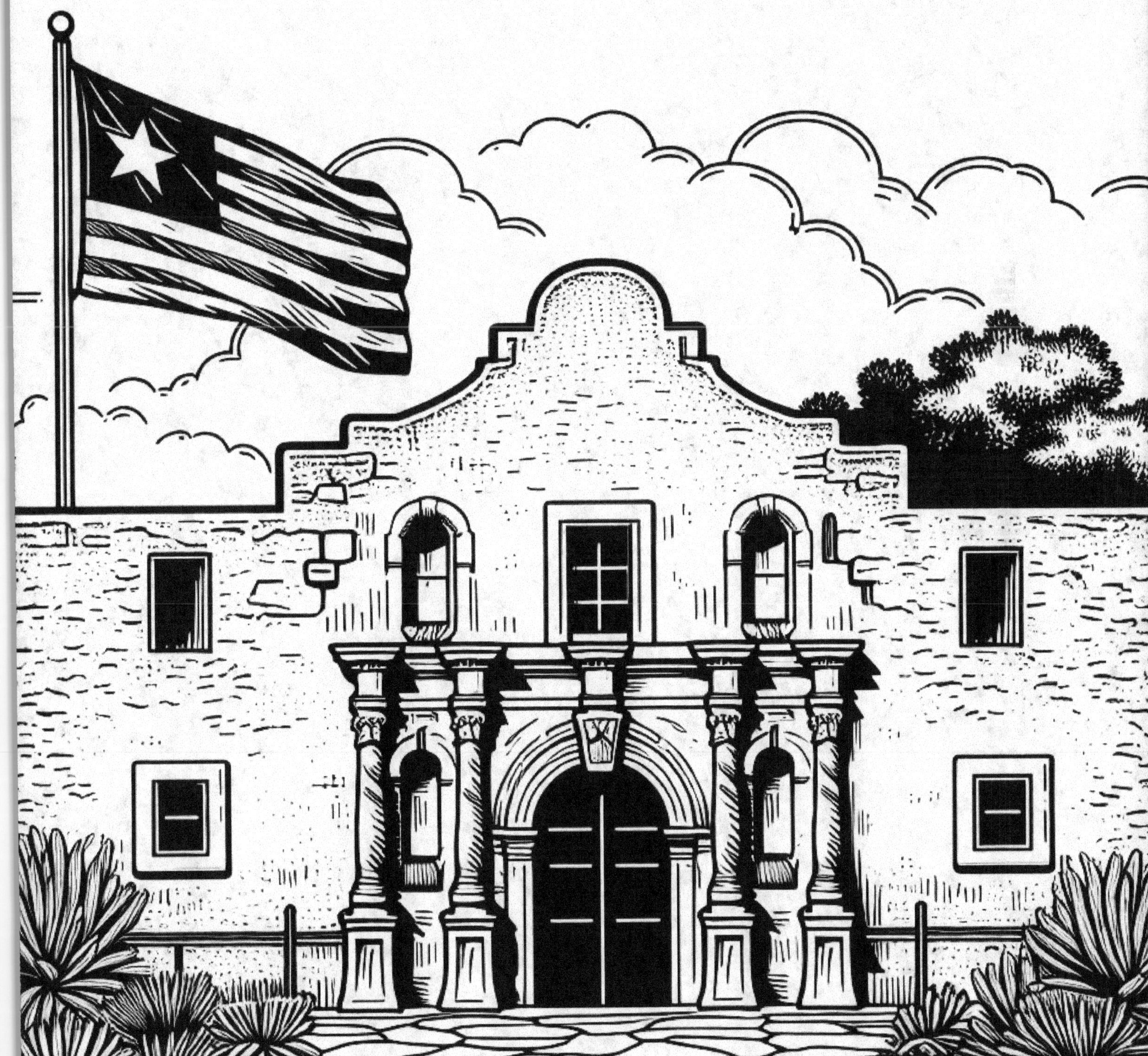

Lincoln Memorial National Monument

Its design was inspired by ancient Greek temples. The architect, Henry Bacon, modeled the memorial after the Greek Doric style, which symbolized the democratic ideals of ancient Greece. The memorial features 36 columns, each representing a state in the Union at the time of Abraham Lincoln's death. Additionally, the interior of the memorial houses a larger-than-life statue of Abraham Lincoln seated in contemplation, sculpted by Daniel Chester French.

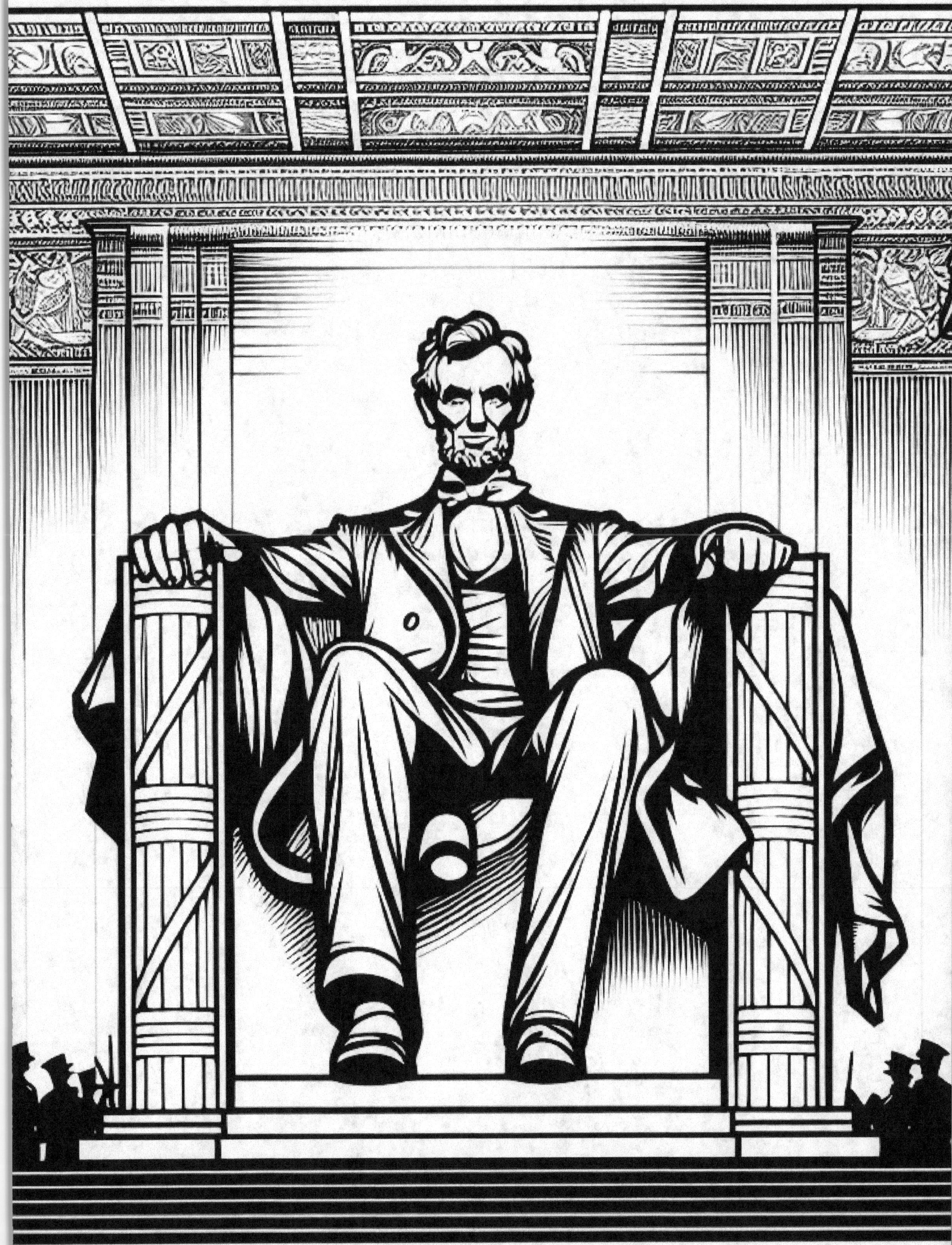

The Golden Gate Bridge, San Francisco, California

Its signature "International Orange" color was originally meant to be a primer, not the final paint color. However, the consulting architect, Irving Morrow, liked the orange hue because it complemented the natural surroundings and enhanced visibility in foggy conditions. Today, its distinctive color has become one of its most iconic features.

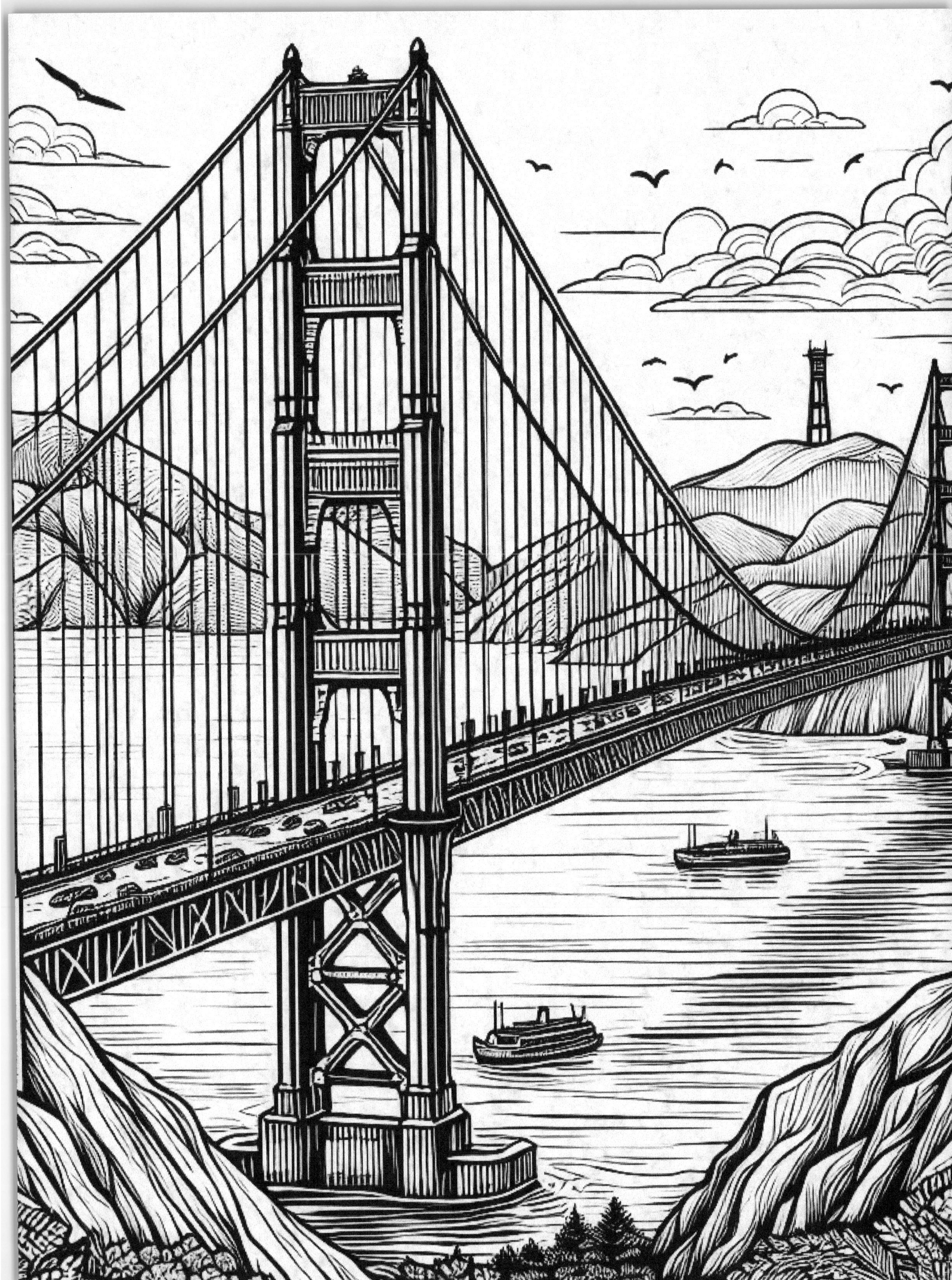

There are some interesting fun facts in American history, let's navigate through some of them

The "Tomatina" incident in 1976, where the city of Buñol, Spain, declared war on the United States in a tomato battle.

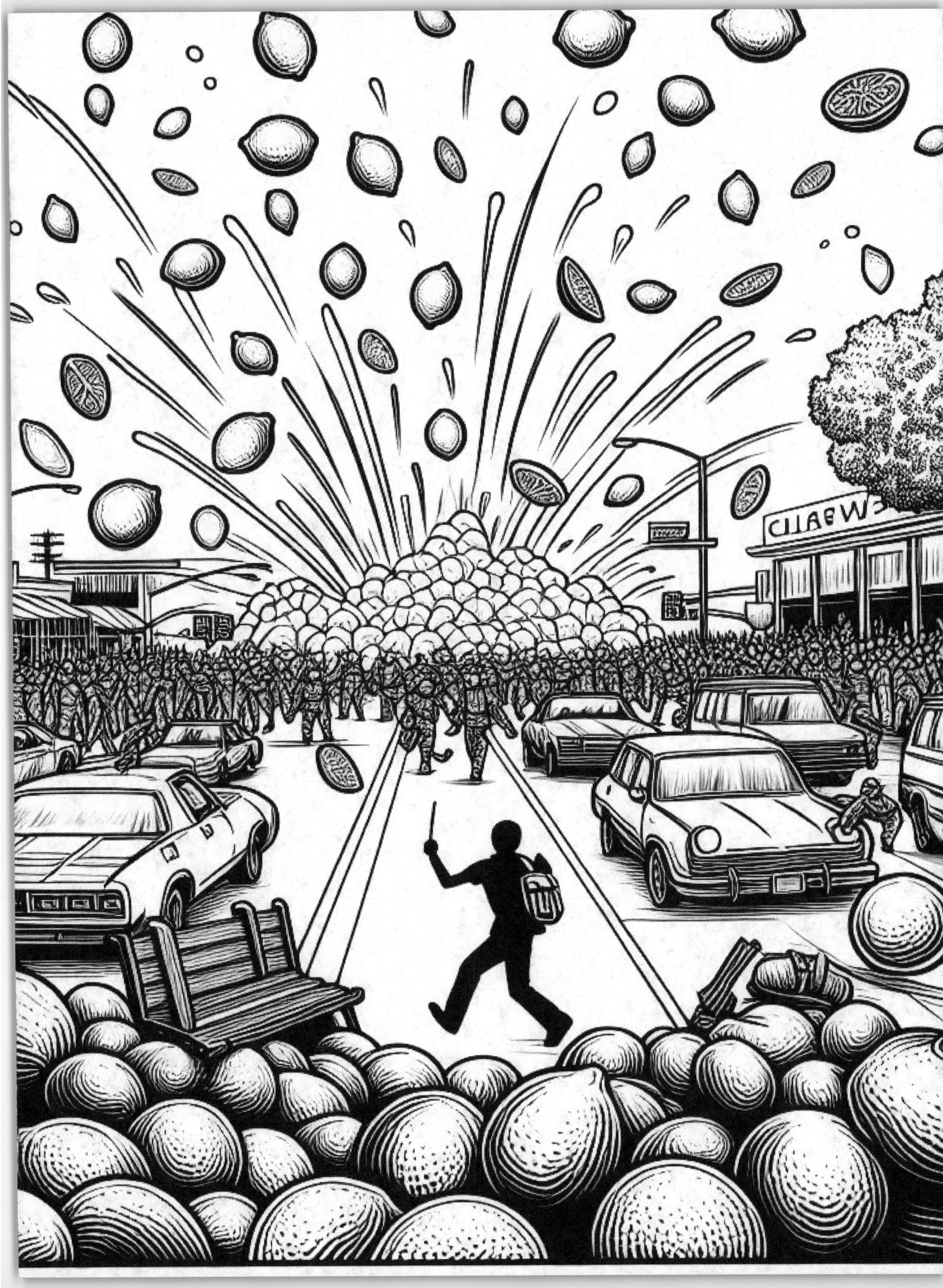

The Niagara Falls is the largest source of hydroelectric power in the world.

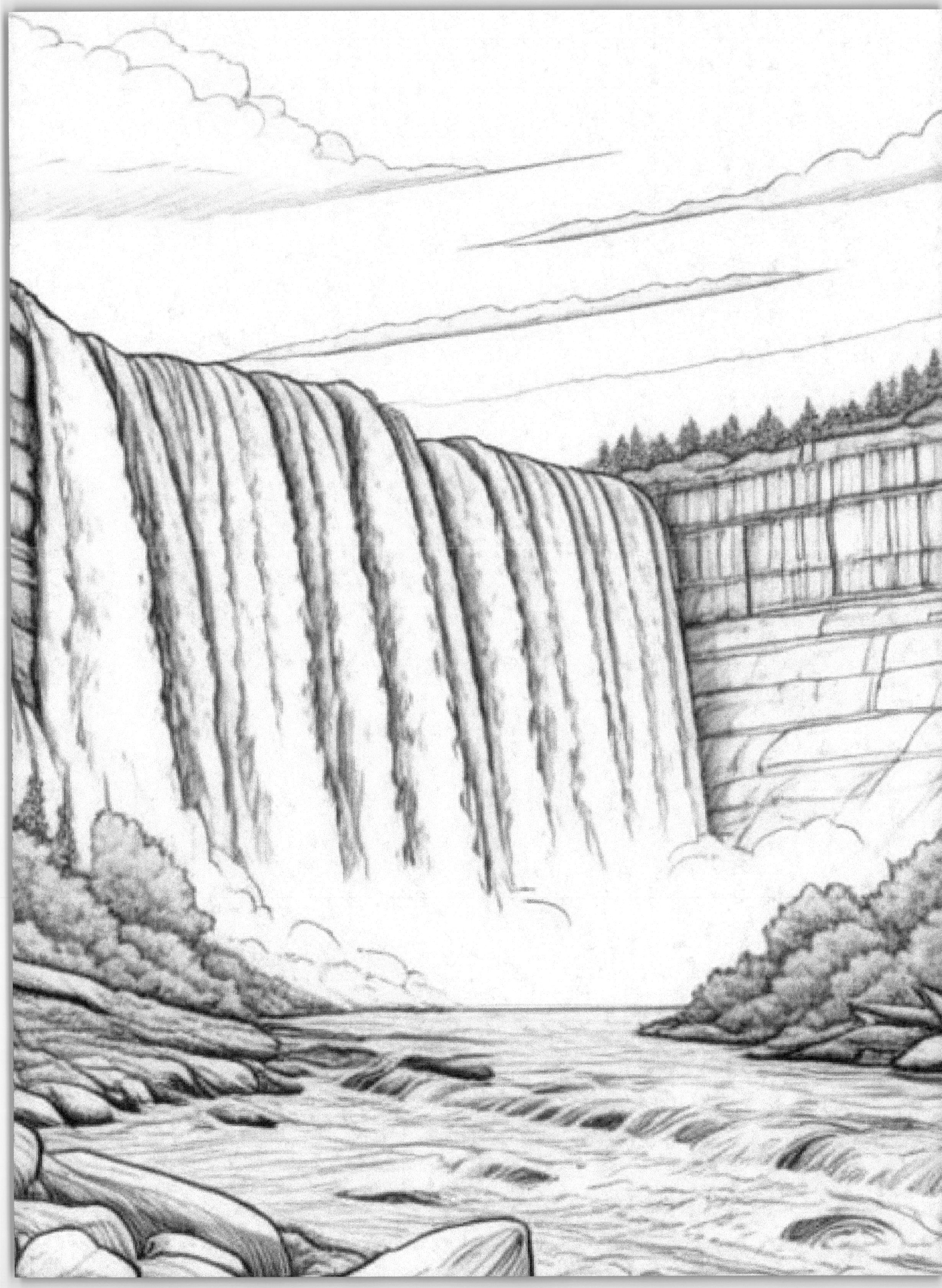

Disneyland theme park in California has over 20,000 trees planted.

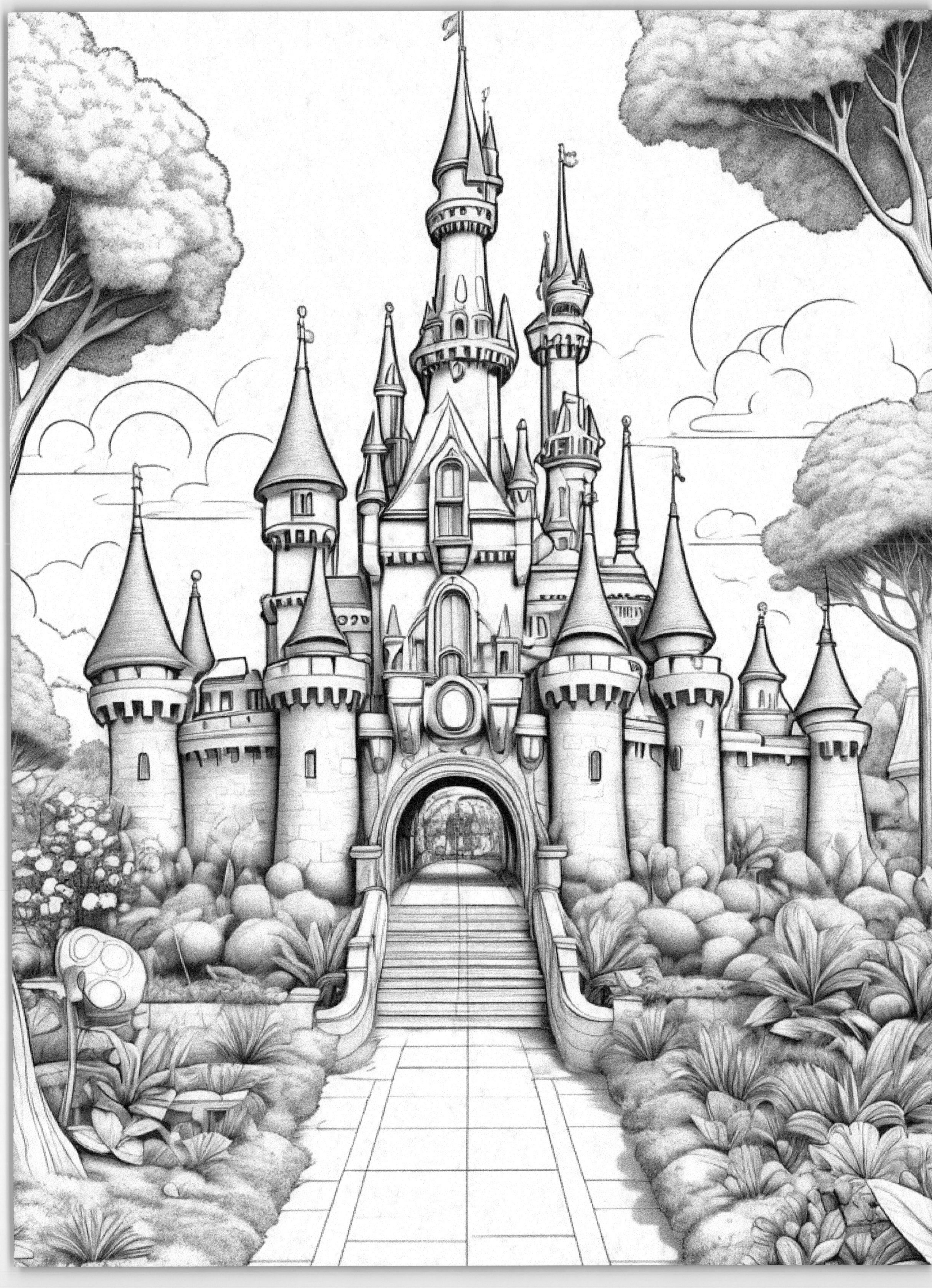

In Texas, there is a law that allows drivers to drive with a cowboy hat.

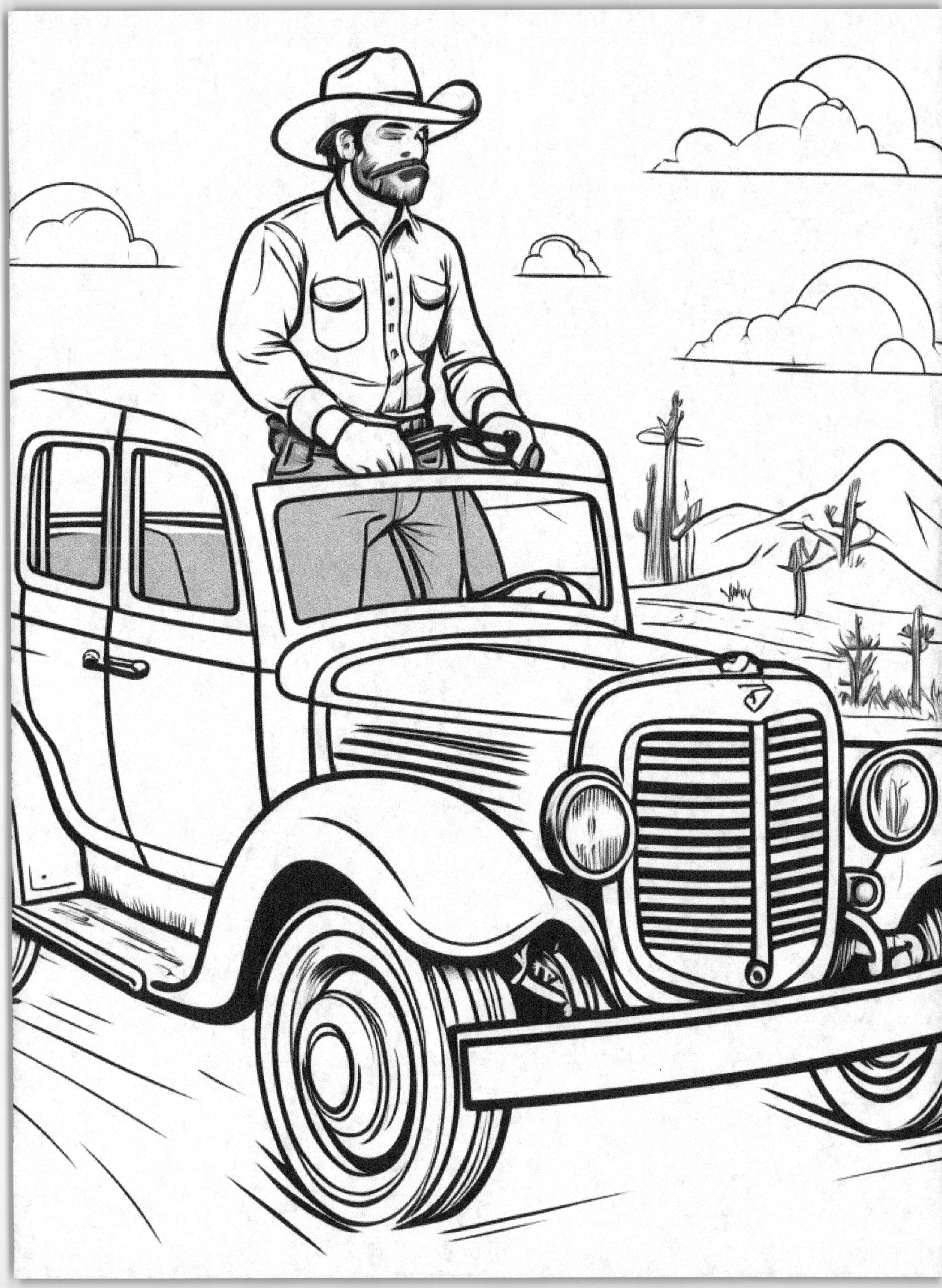

Mount McKinley, also known as Denali, is the tallest mountain in North America.

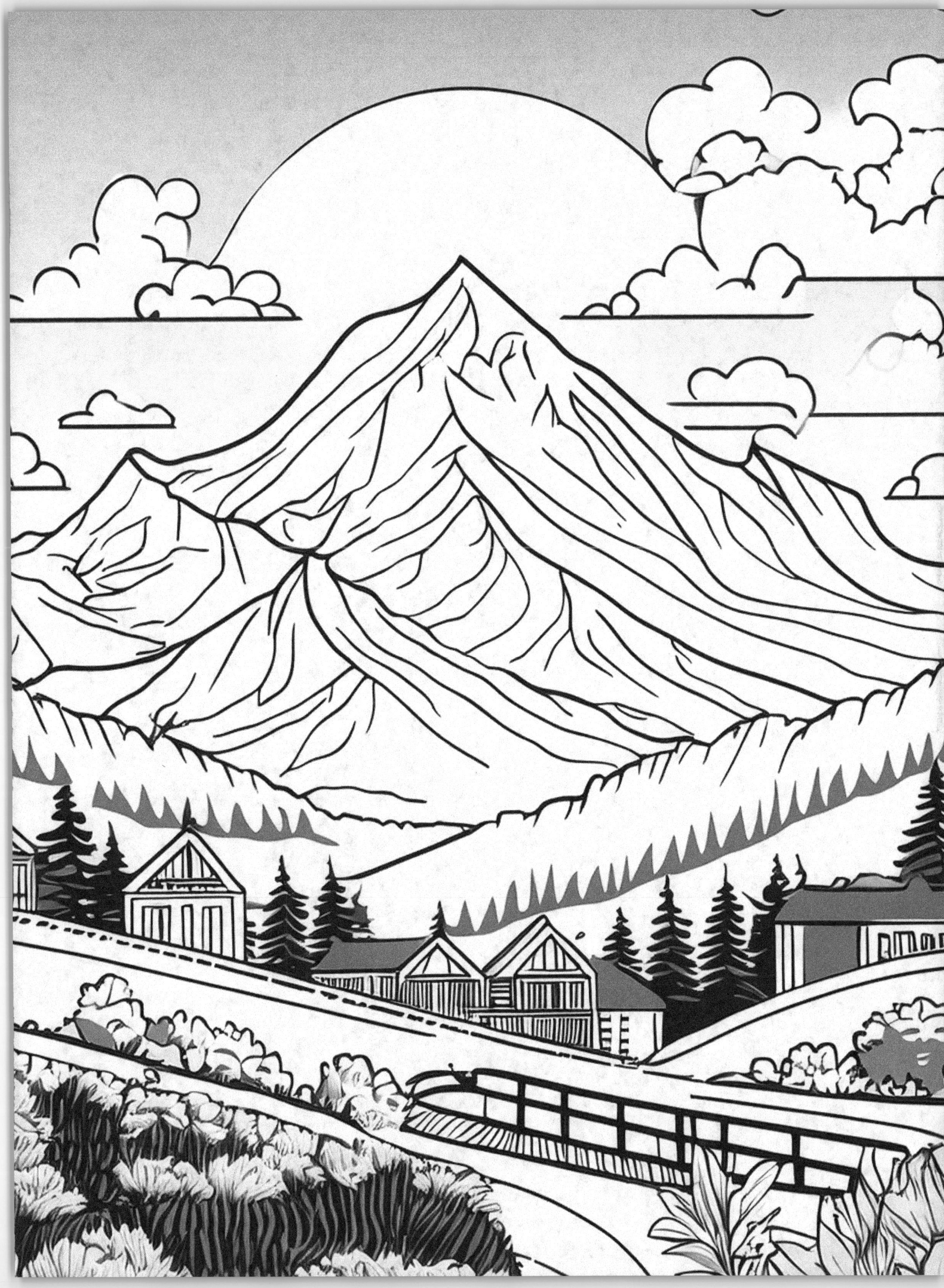

The premiere of the television series "The Simpsons" in 1989, which has become one of the longest-running and beloved in history.

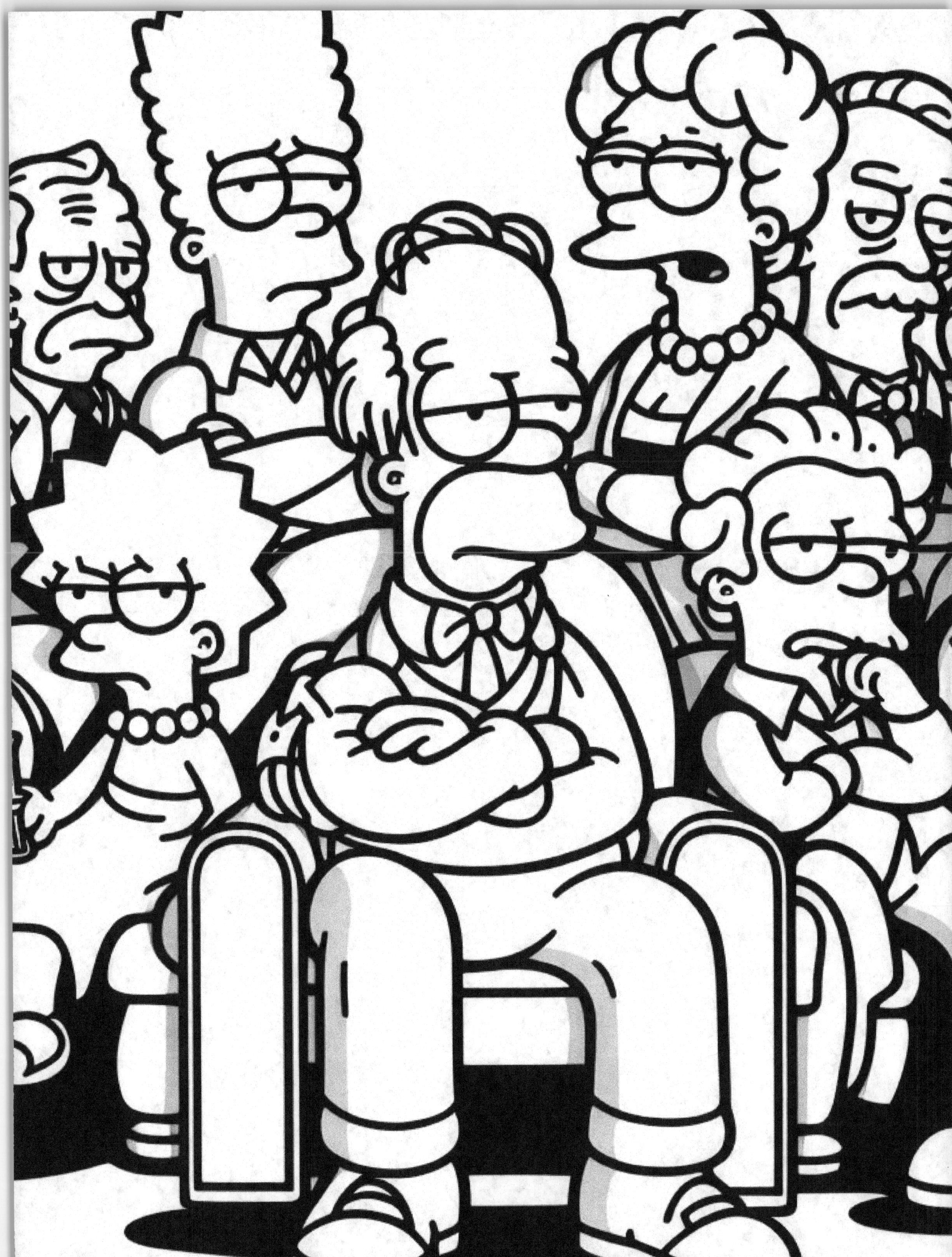

The National Museum of Natural History in Washington D.C. houses the world's largest collection of dinosaur bones

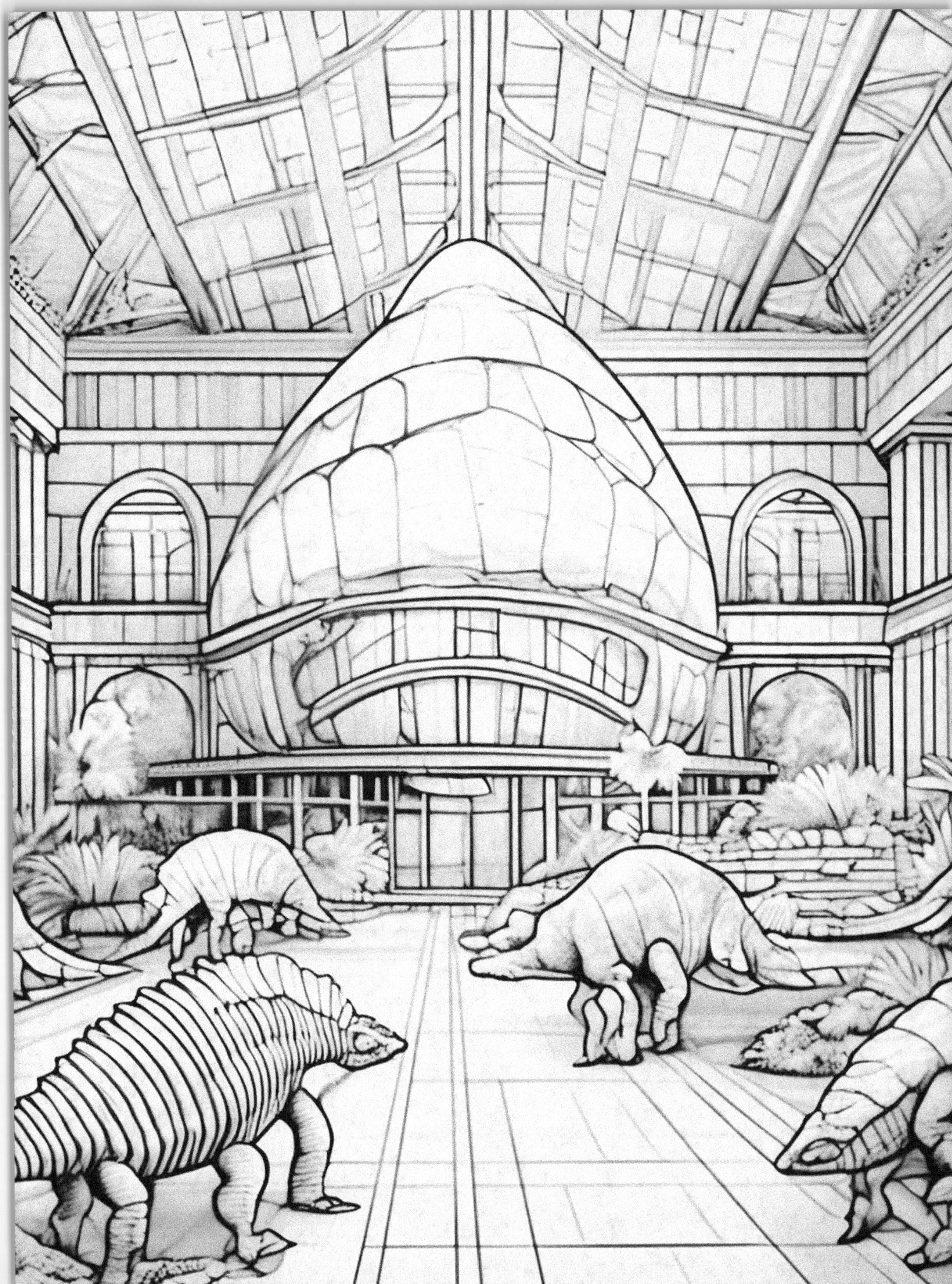

Okay, they say the best part of the cake is saved for last, time to enjoy some relaxing and beautiful mandalas.

Gray Wolf Mandala

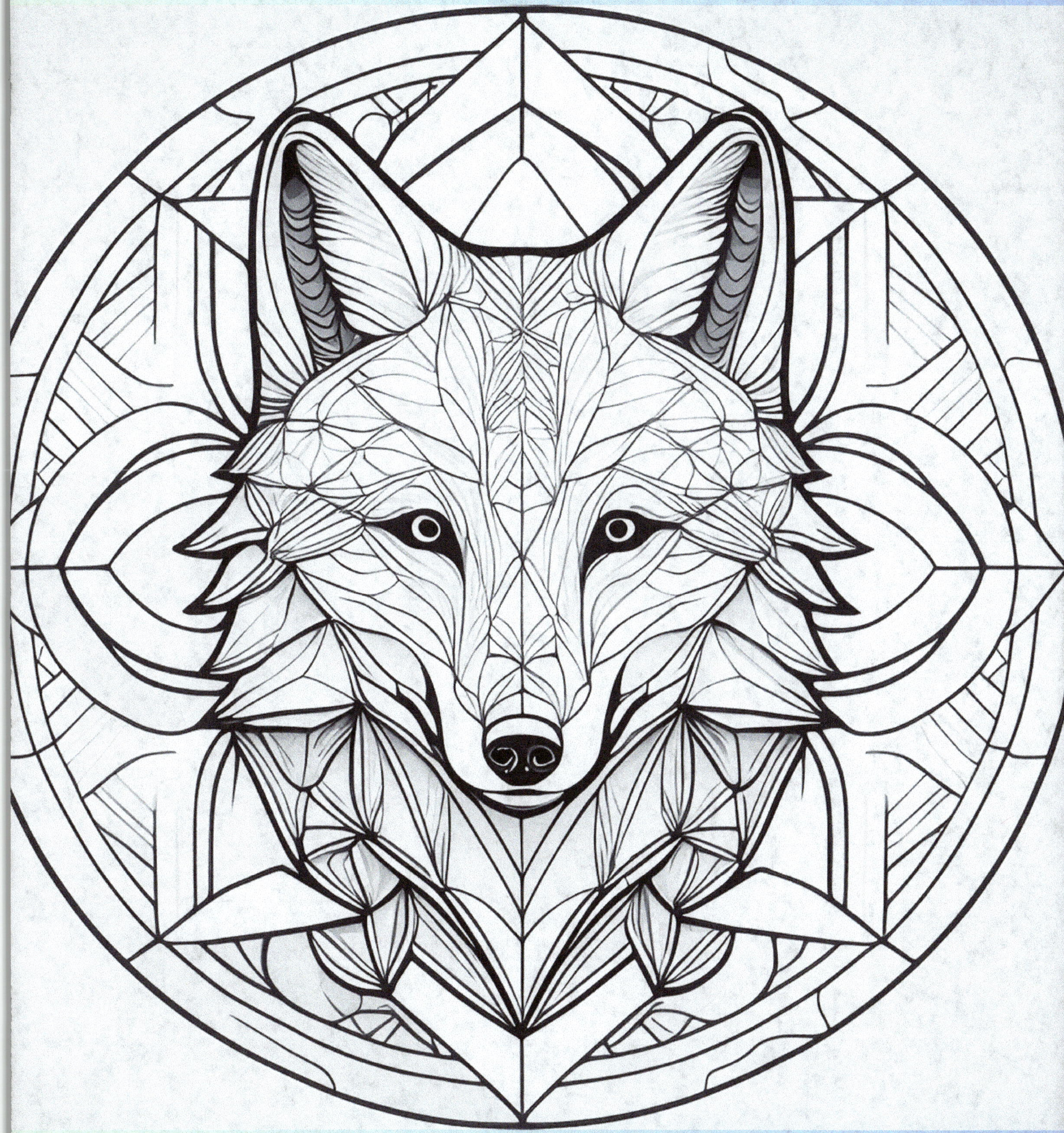

Gray Wolf Mandala in negative

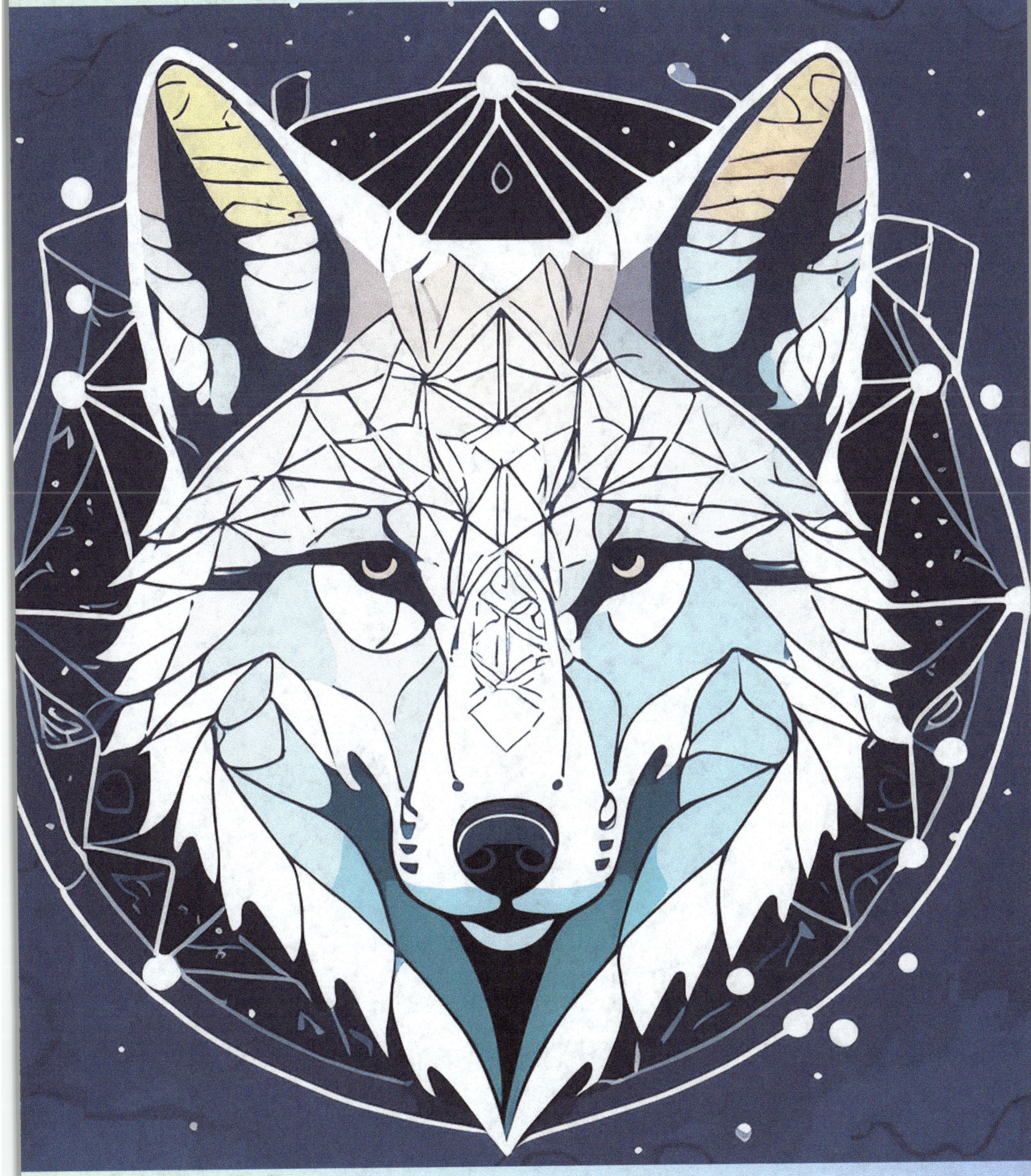

Spacial Red Fox Mandala

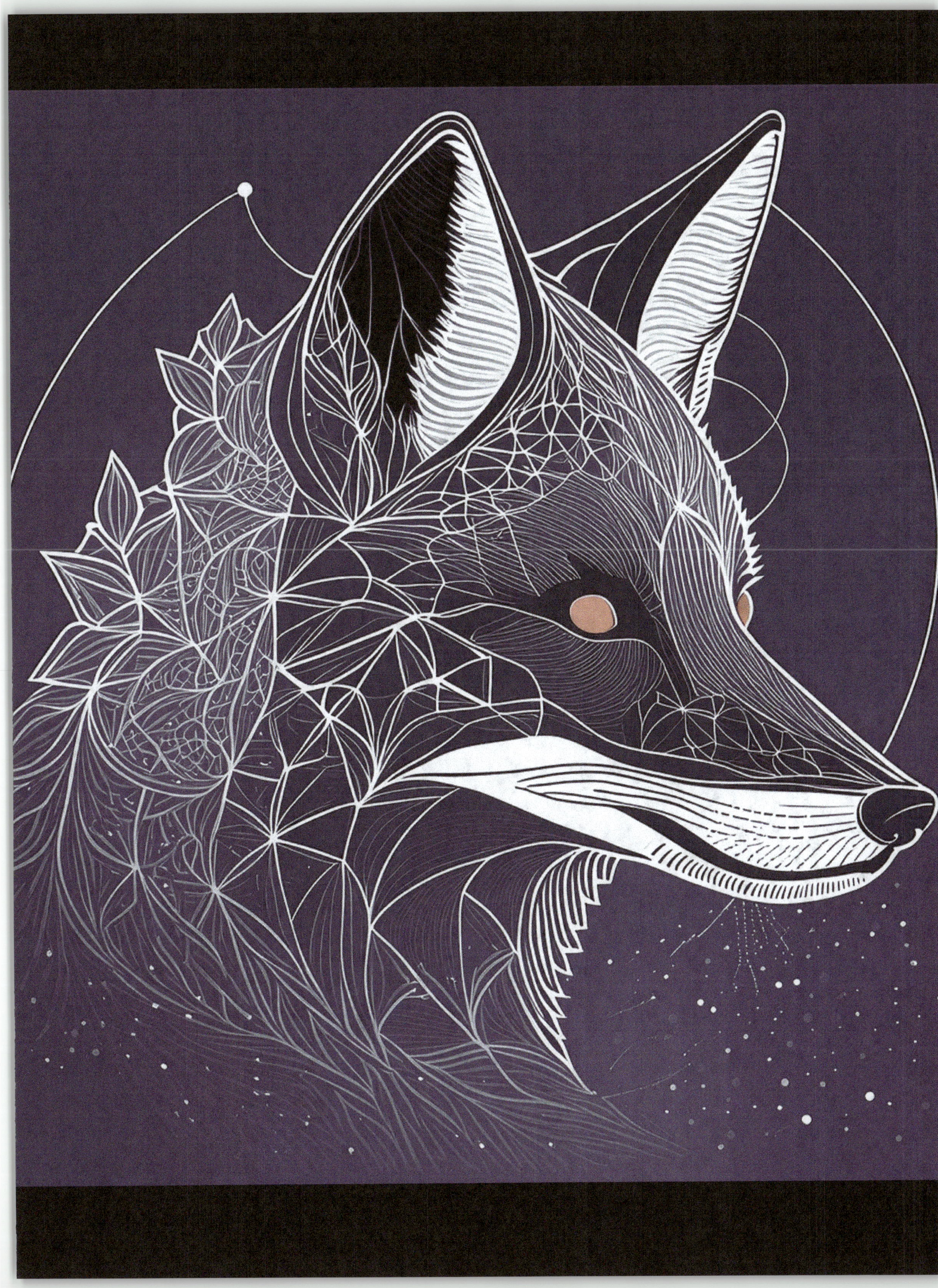

Moose Mandala

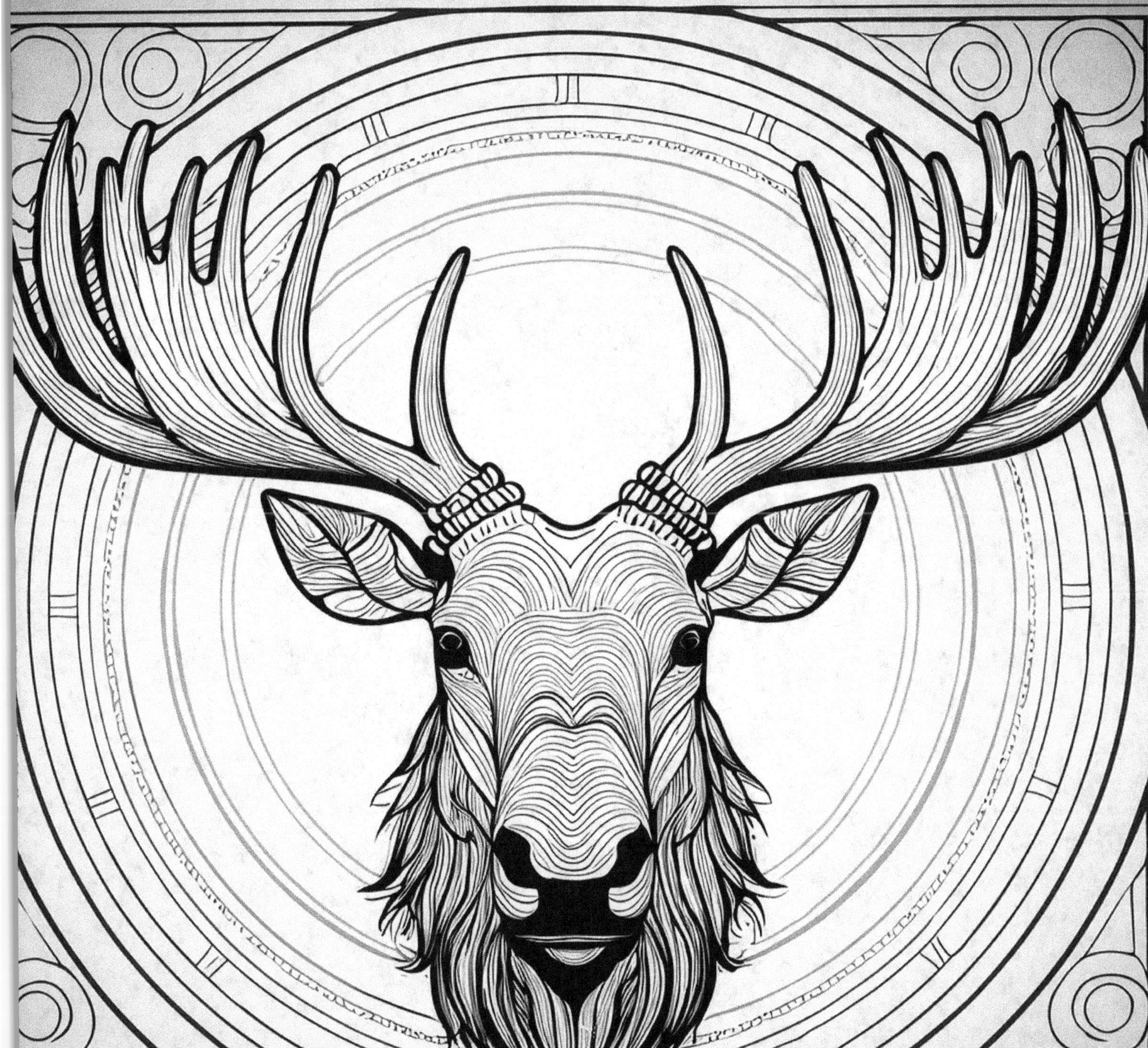

Mandala with mirror design and perfect symmetry

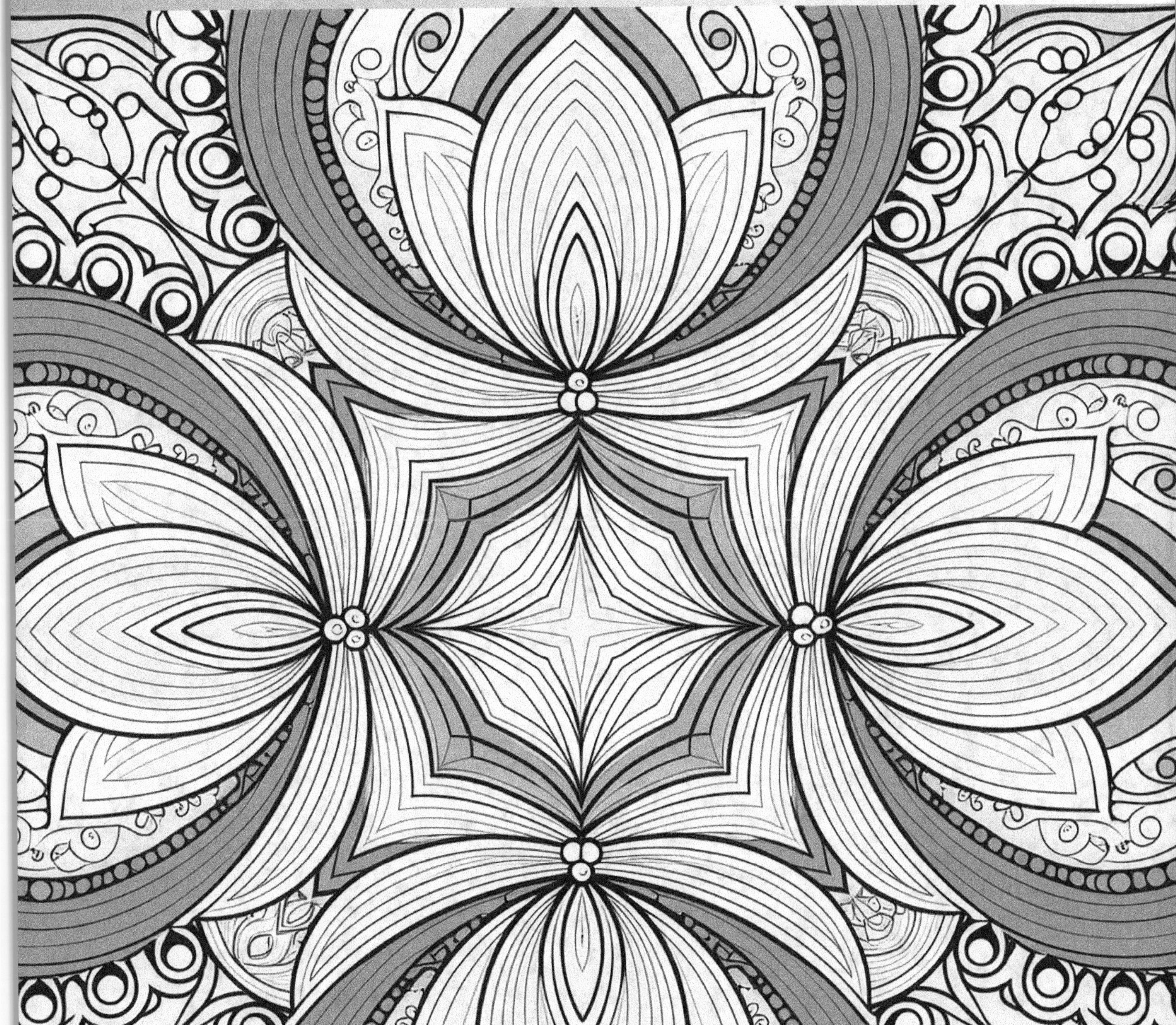

Mandala withClocks and gears design

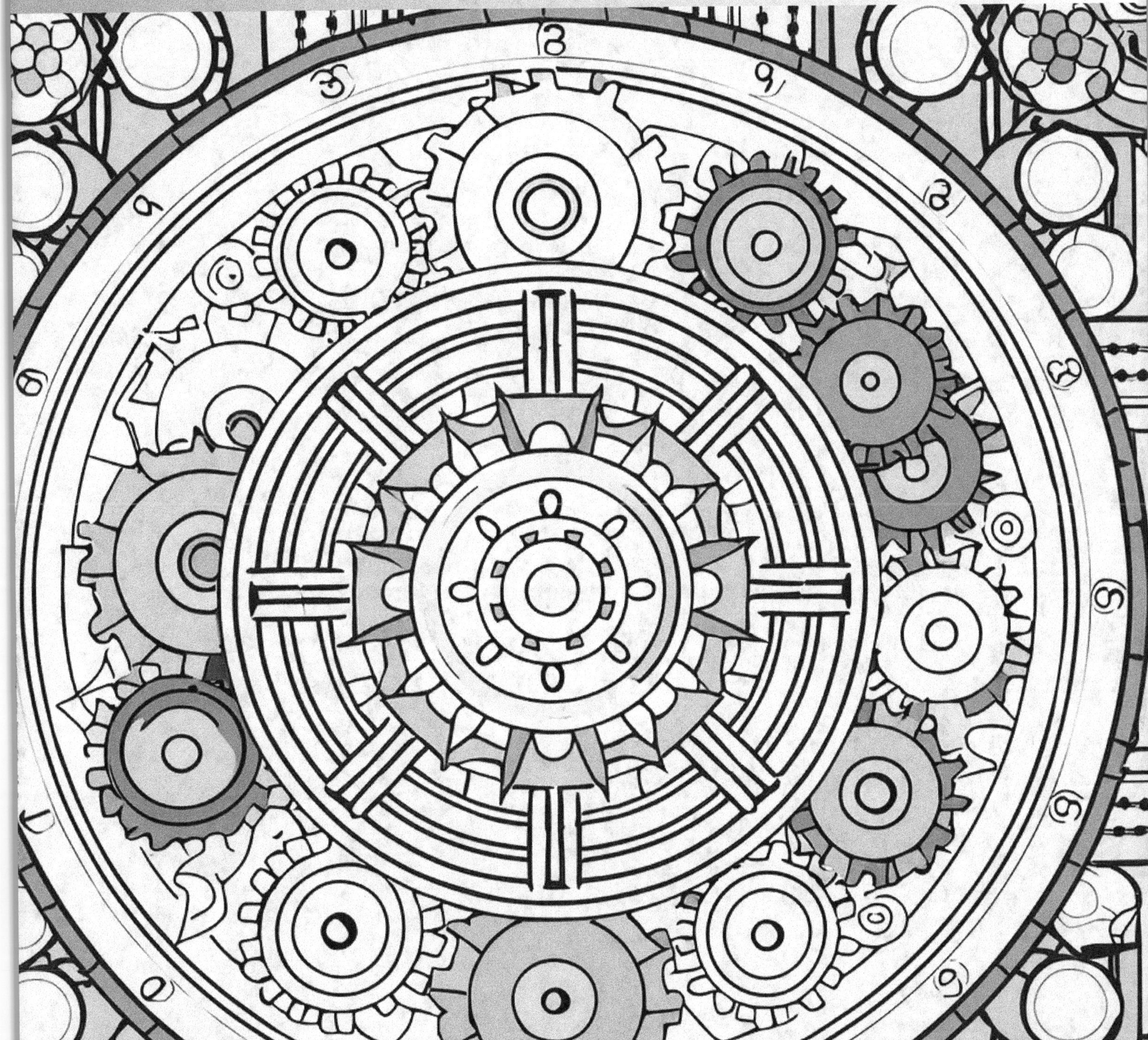

Mandala with fractal design and sacred geometry

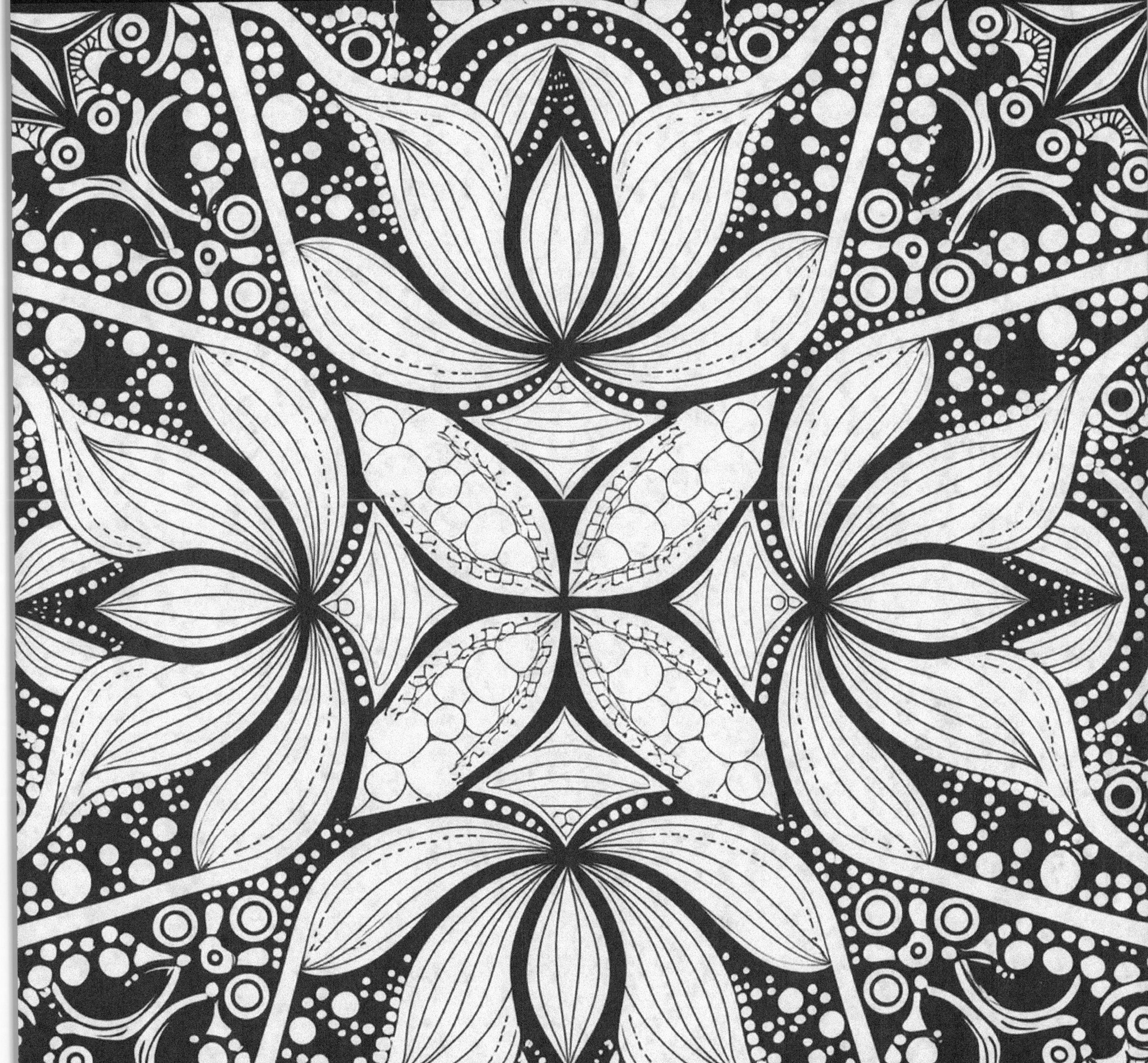

Mandala with diamonds design and perfect symmetry

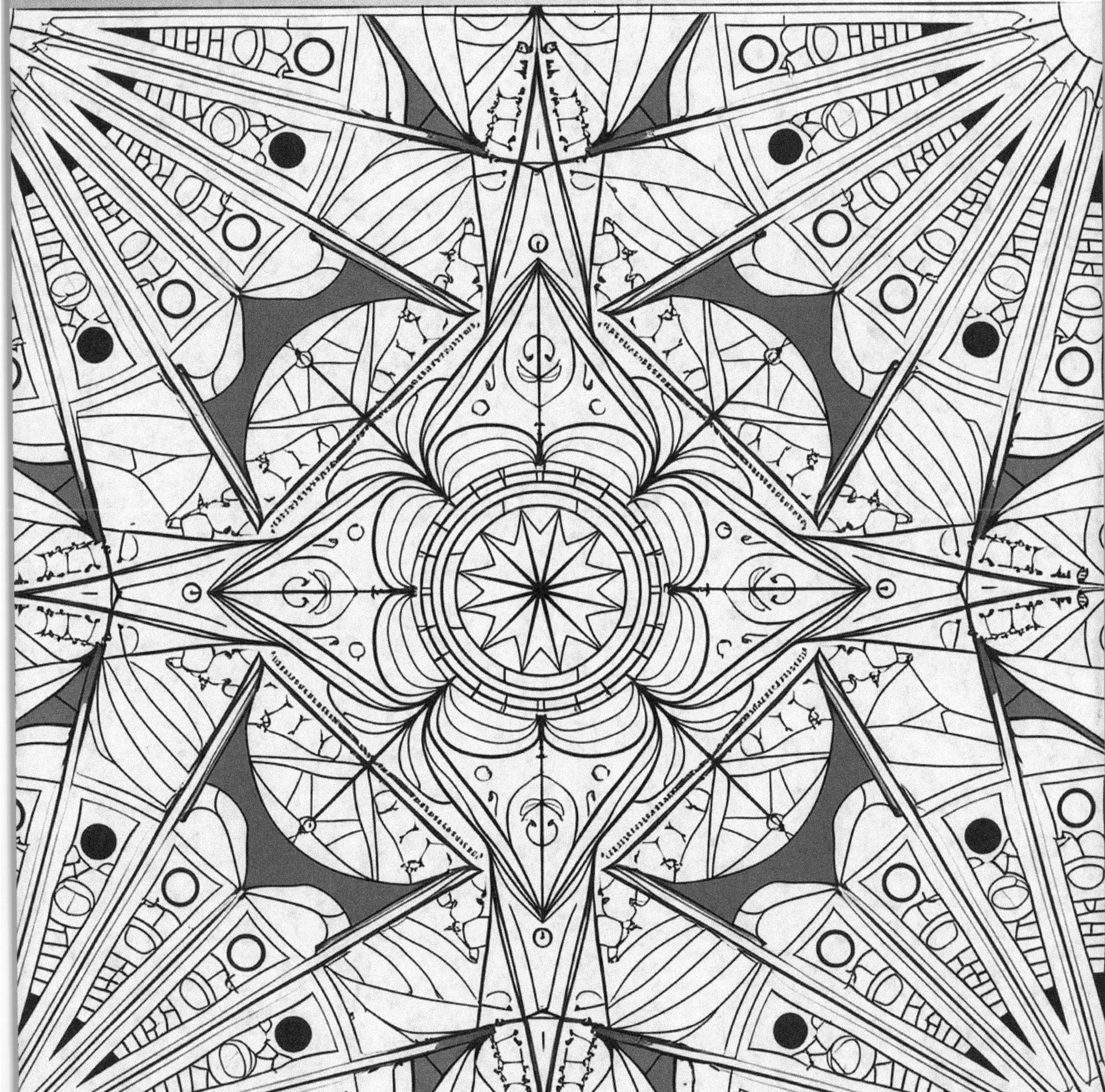

Mandala with bird motifs

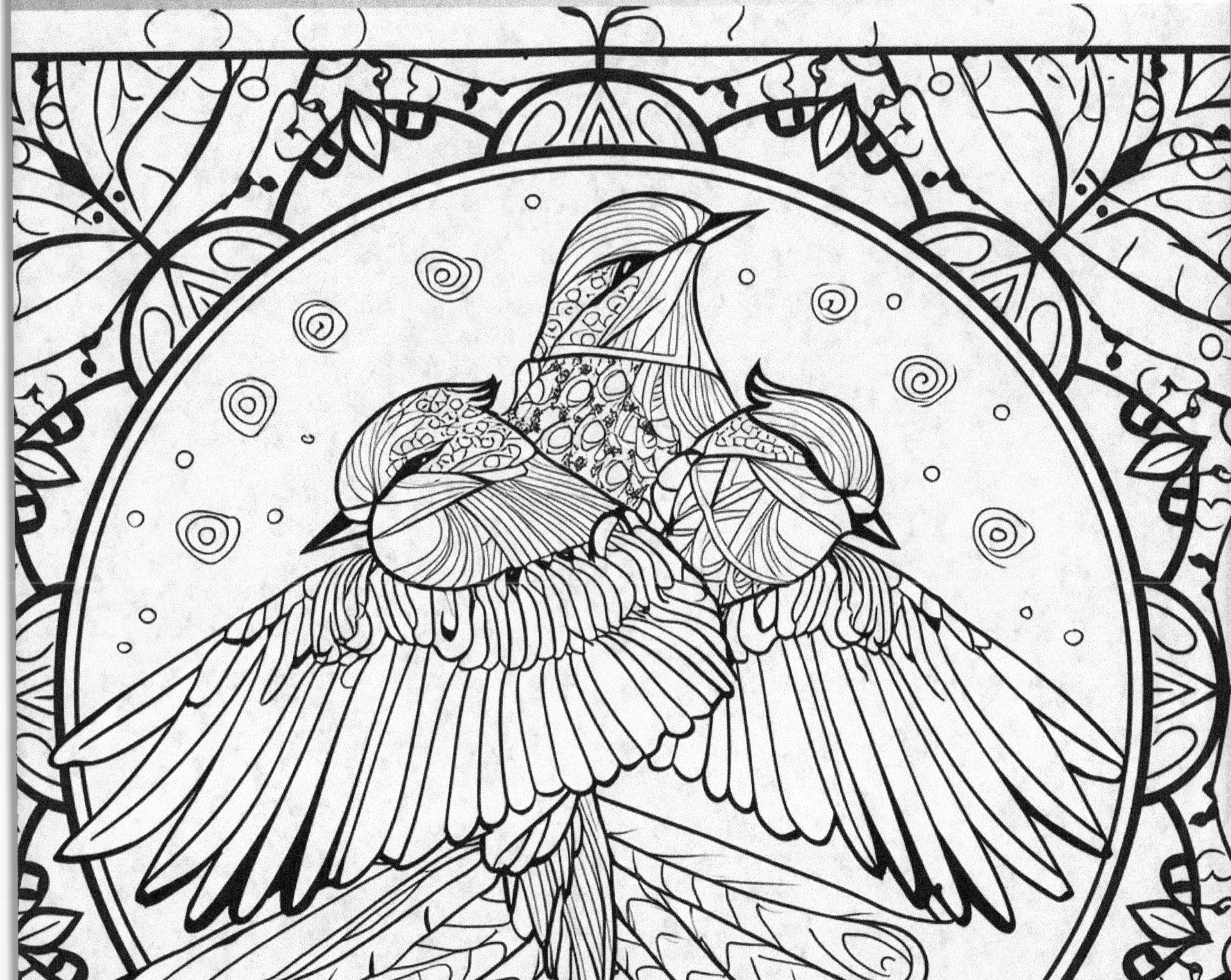

Mandala with butterfly motifs

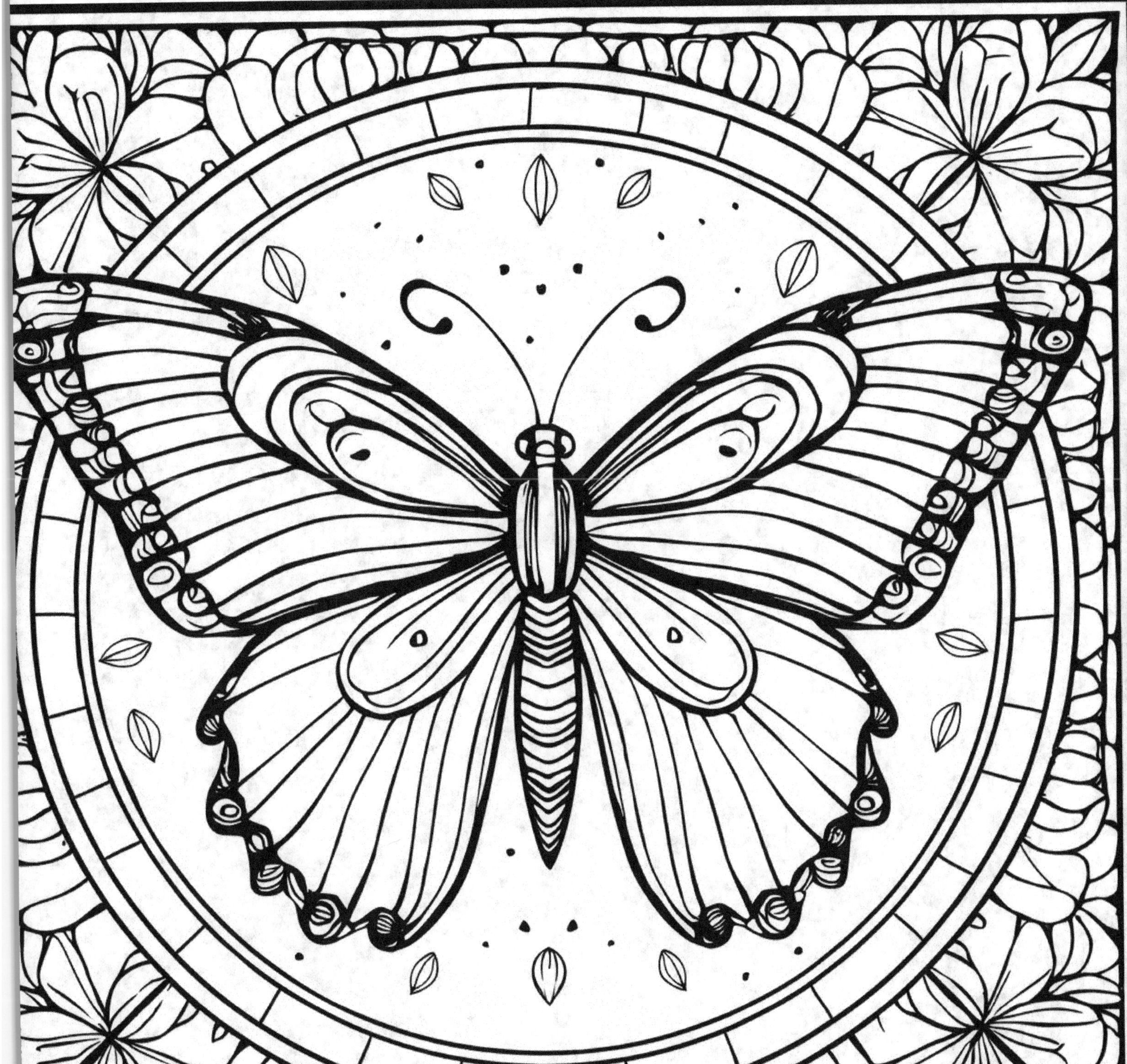

Mandala with motifs inspired by leaves and branches

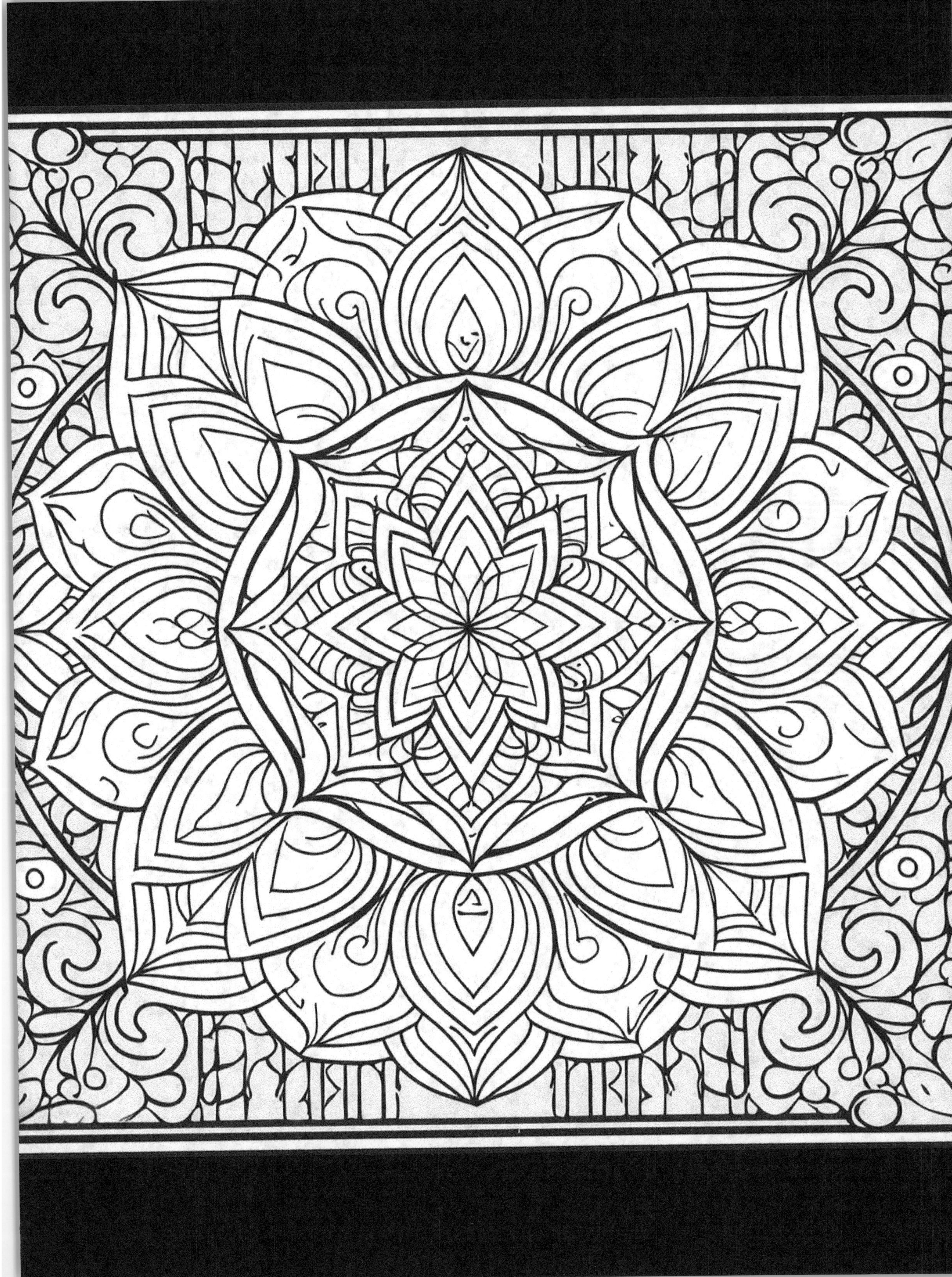

Mandala with floral patterns in concentric layers

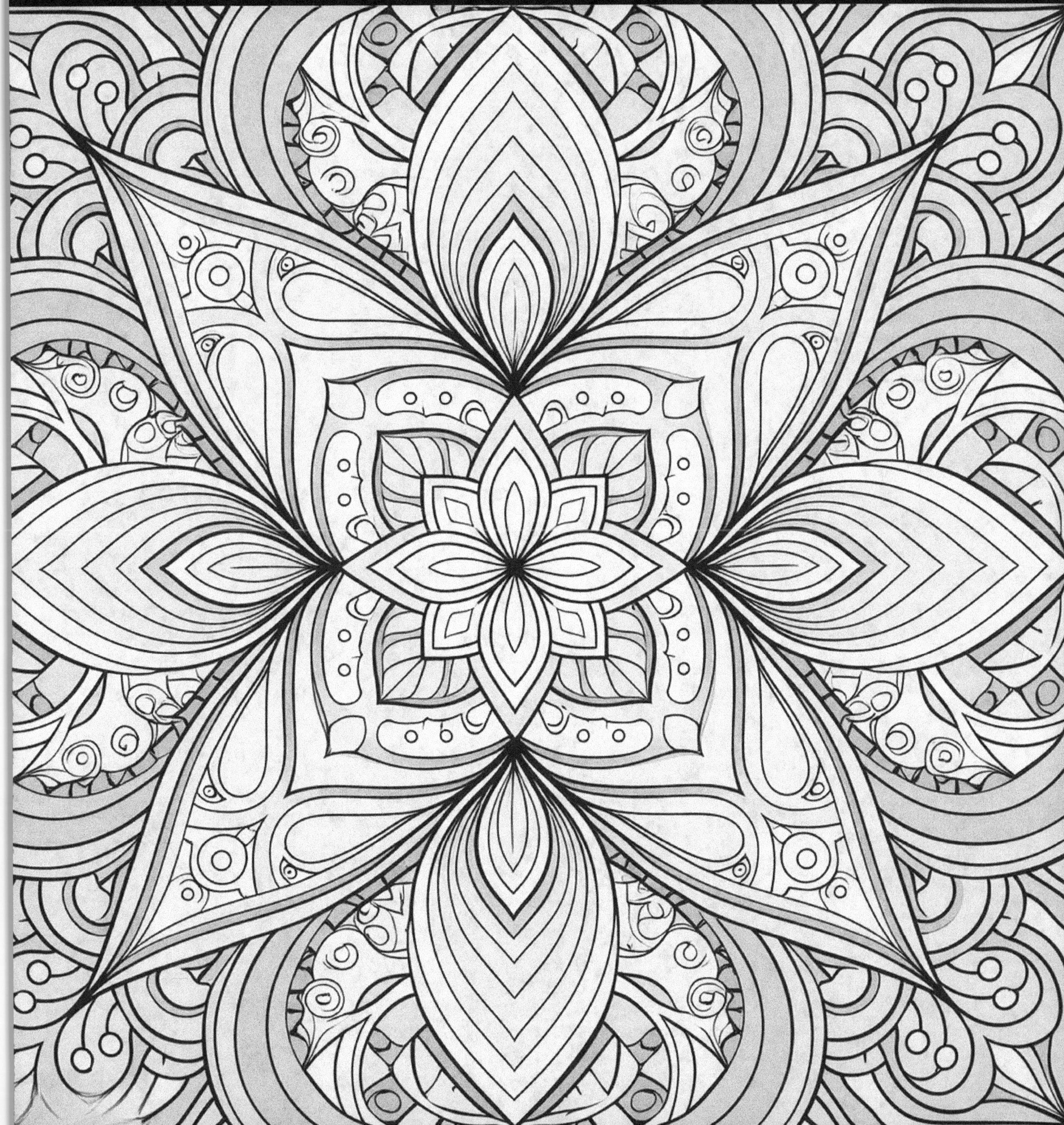

Mandala with floral patterns in concentric layers

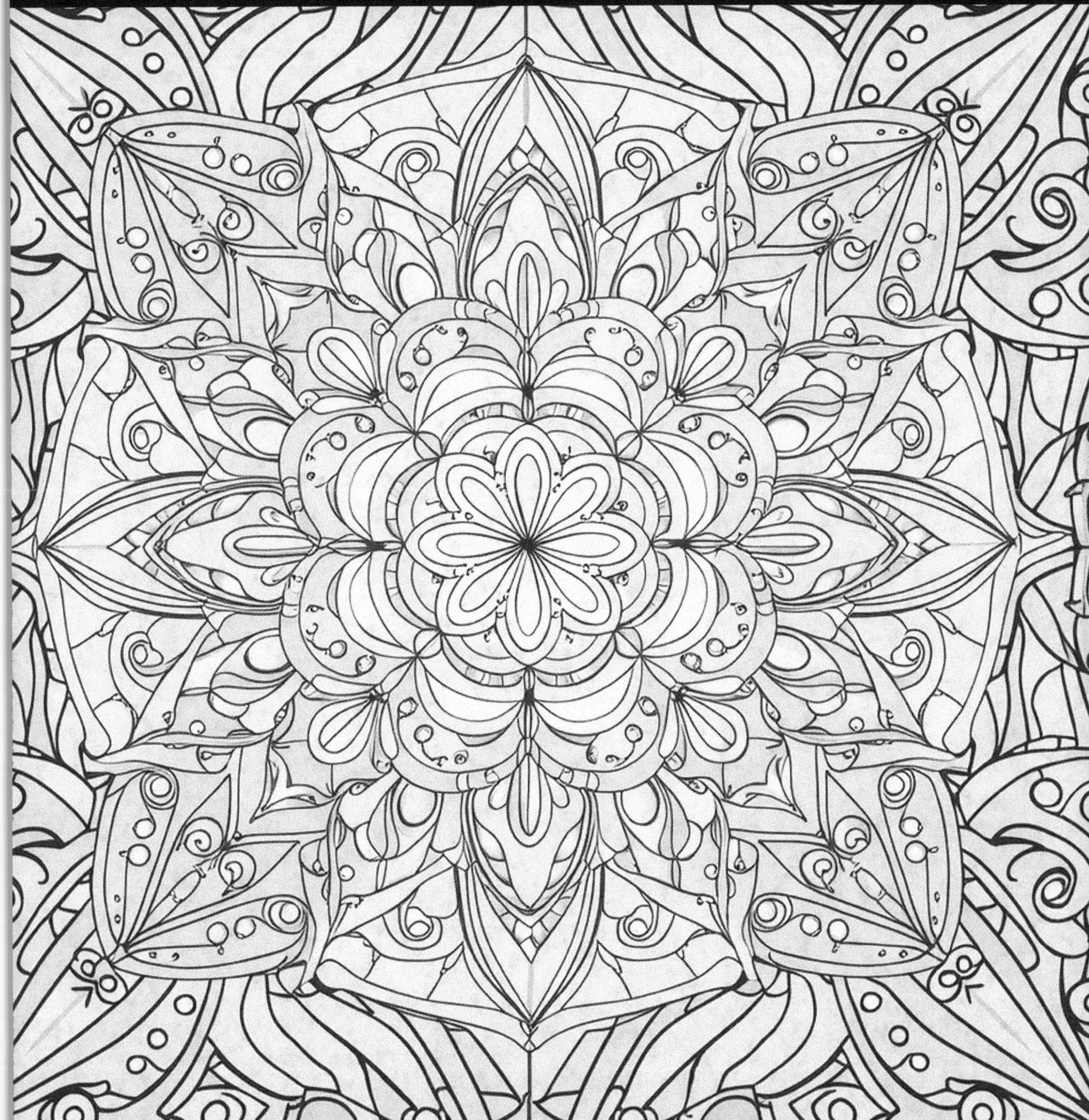

Mandala with motifs of musical instruments and notes

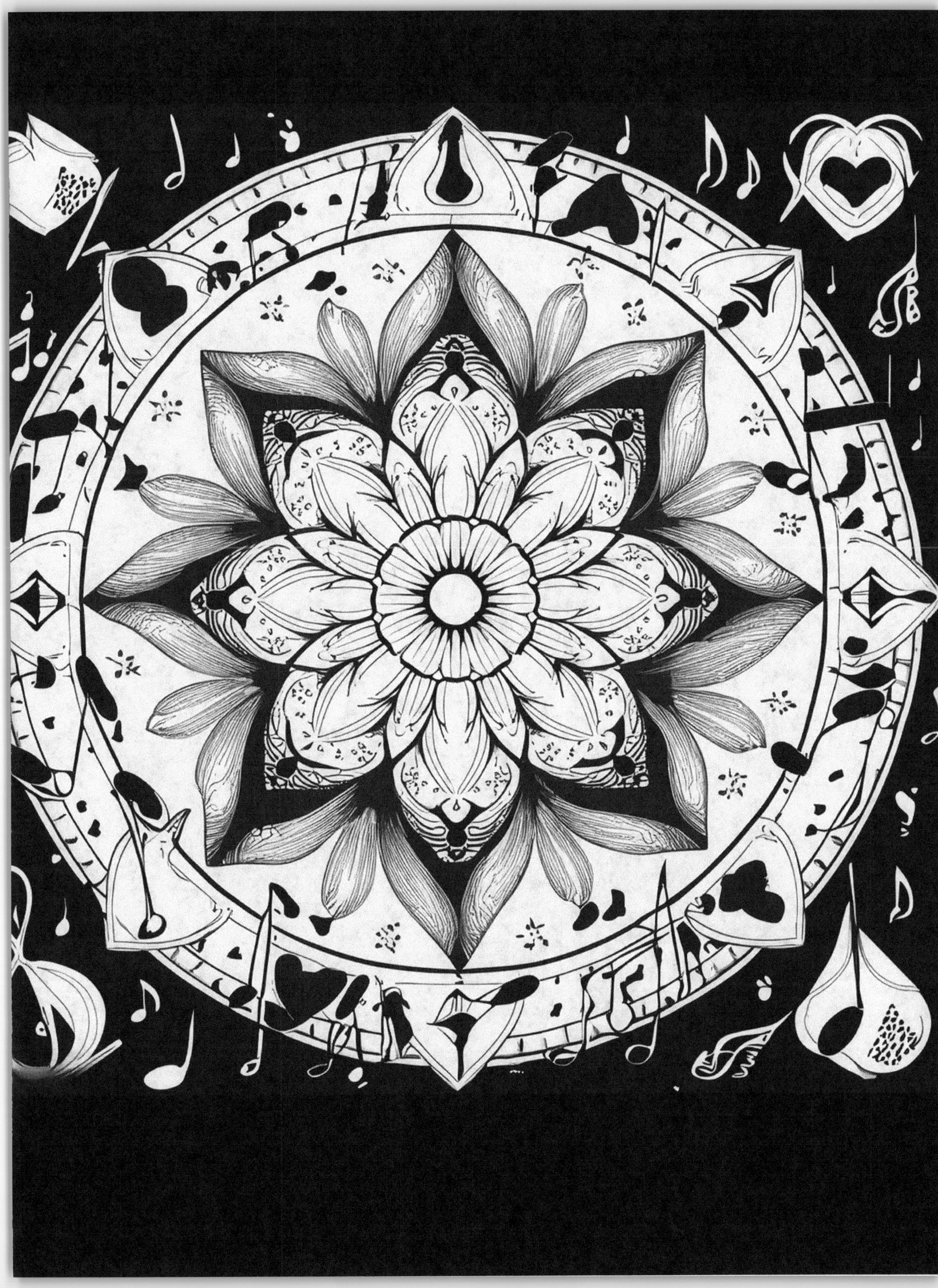

Wild Turkey Mandala

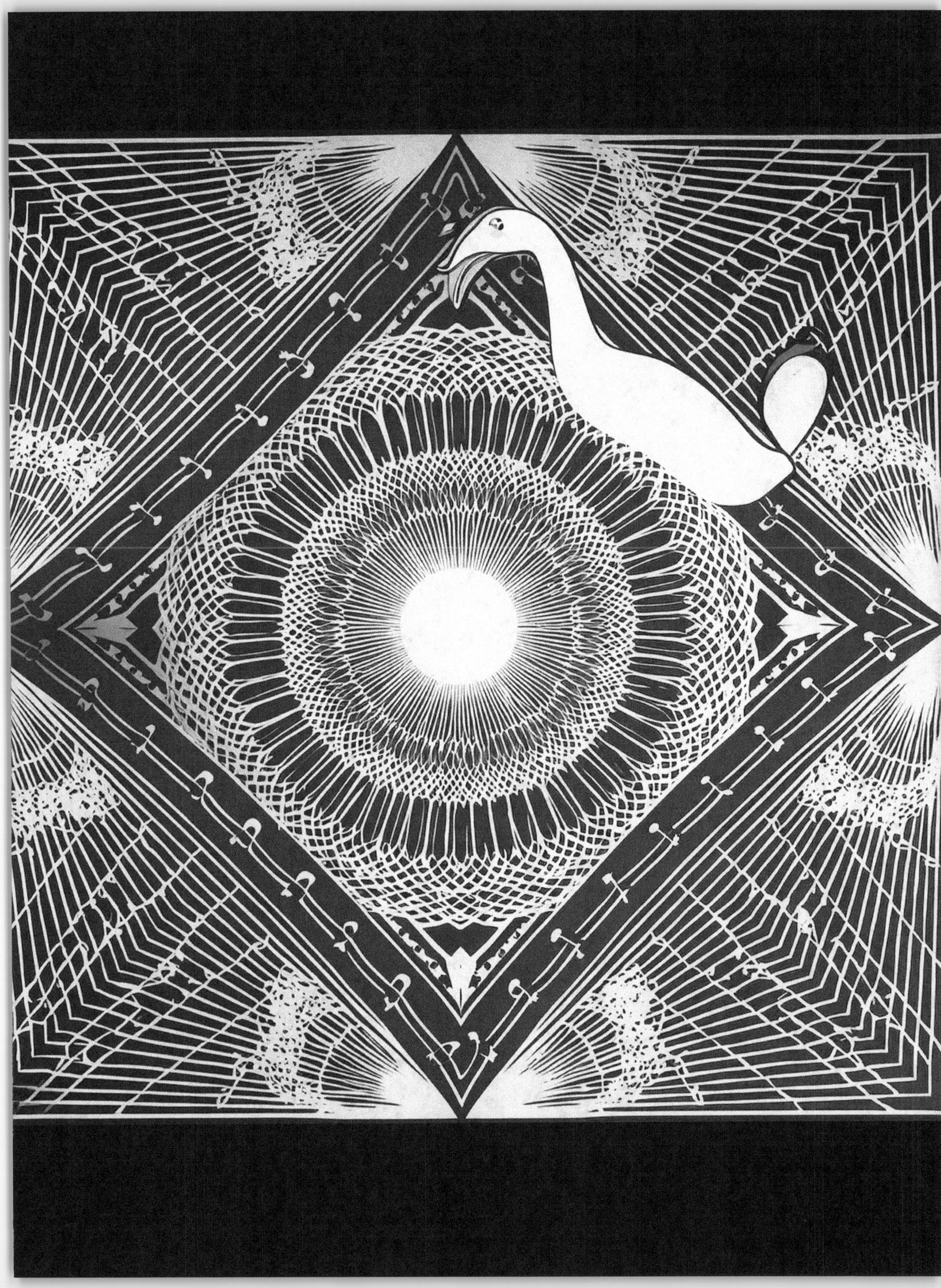

Spacial Grizzly Bear Mandala

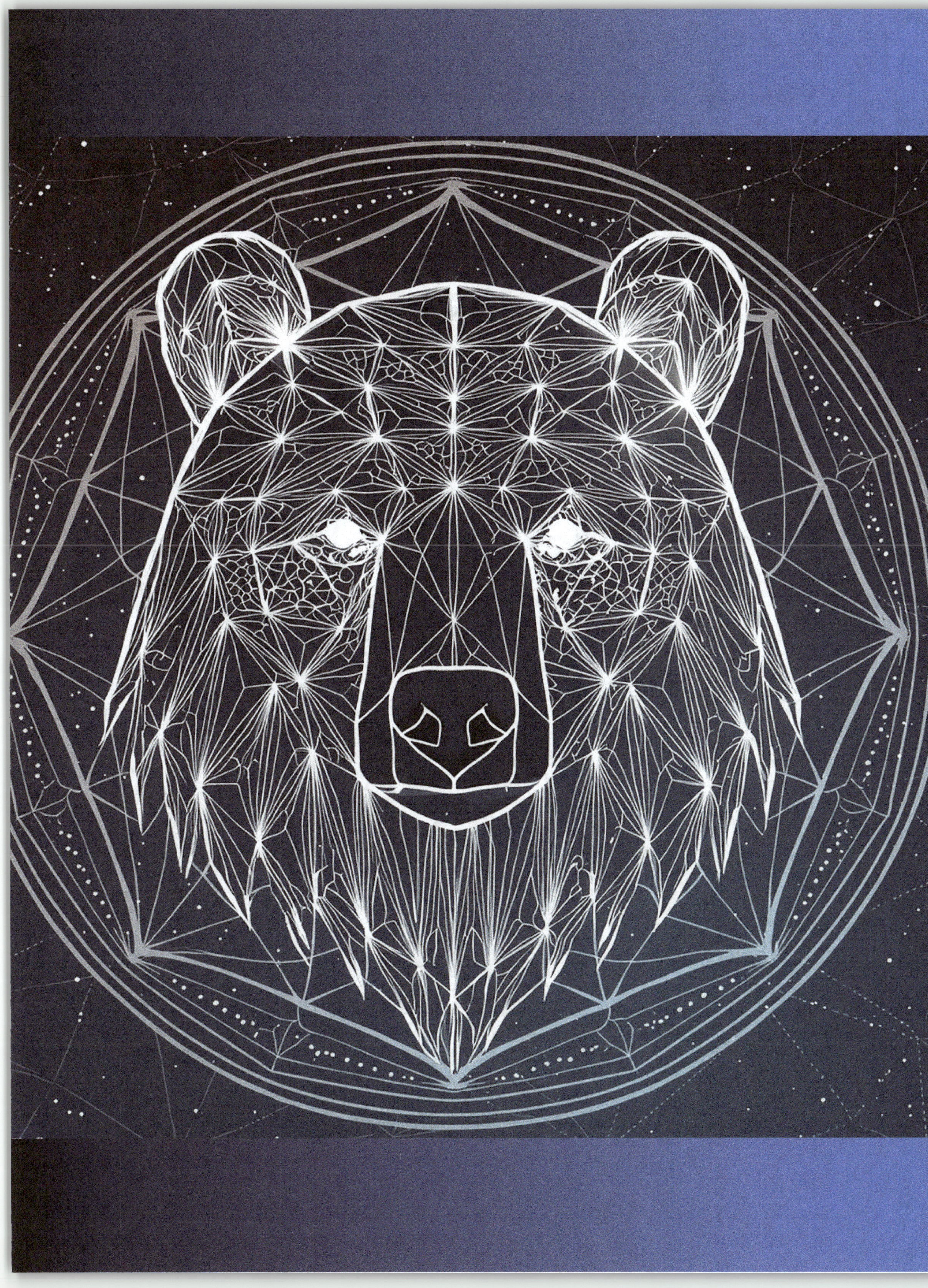

Sacred Grizzly Bear Mandala

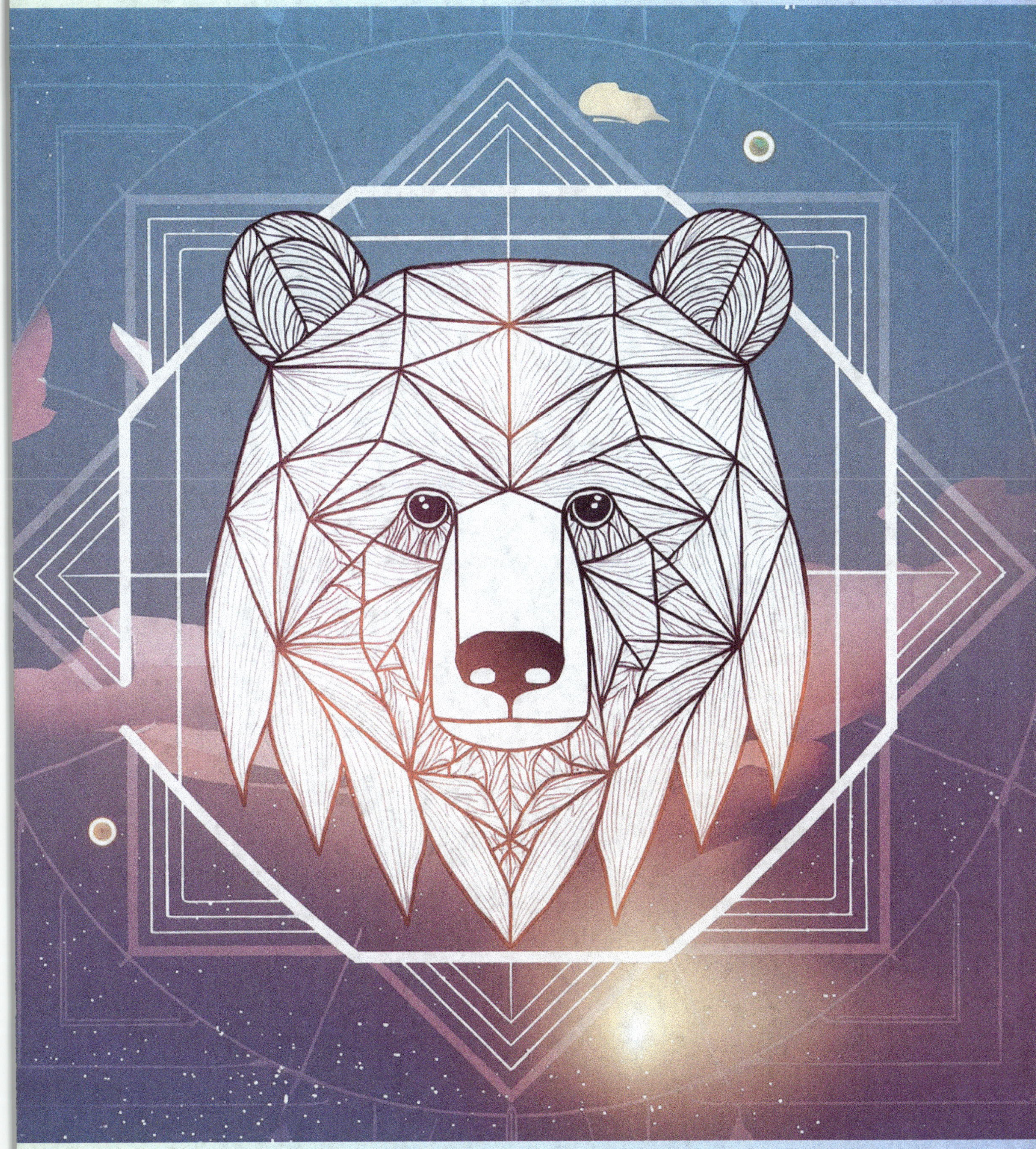

Sacred White-tailed Deer Mandala

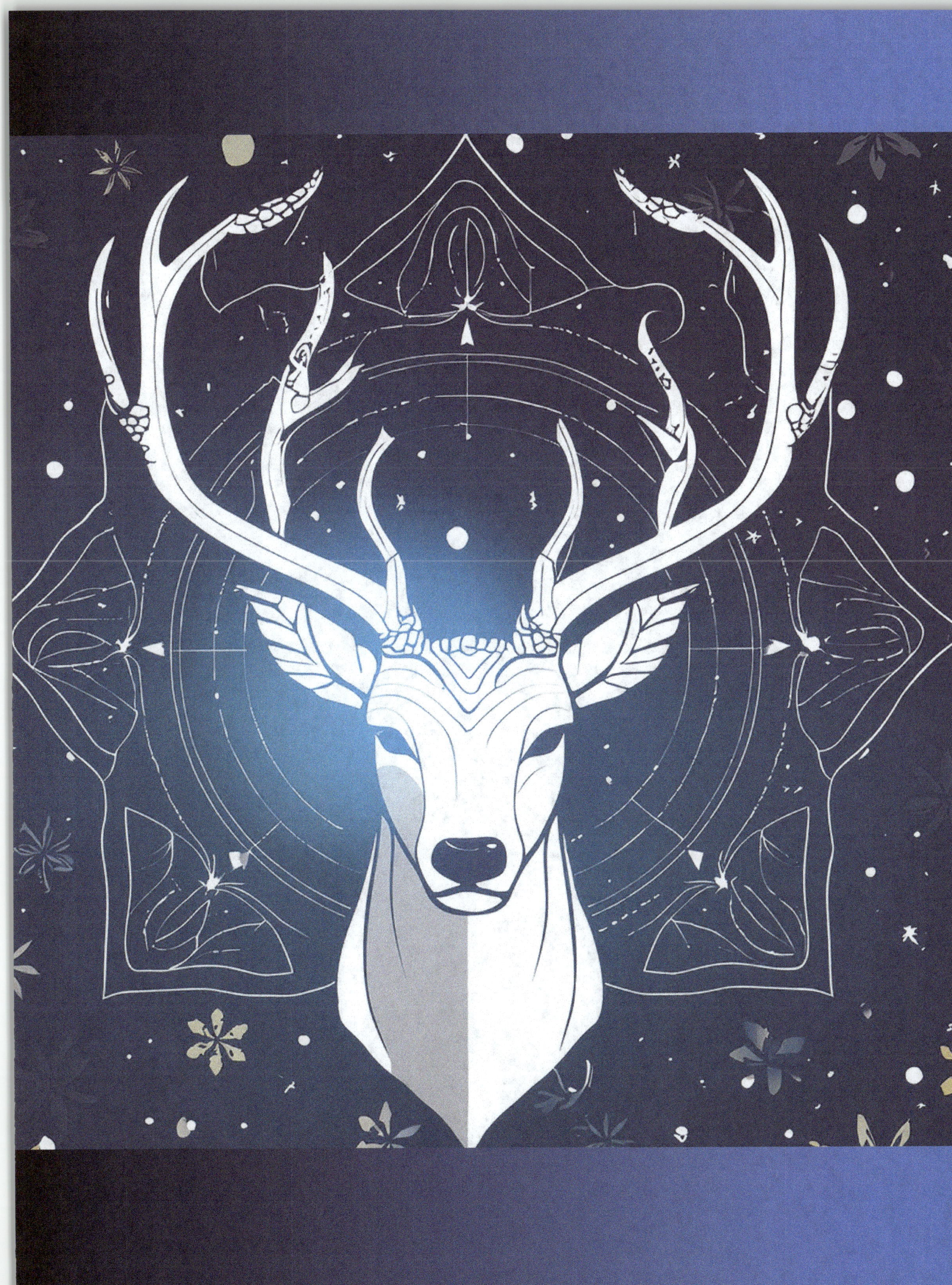

White-tailed Deer Mandala in negative

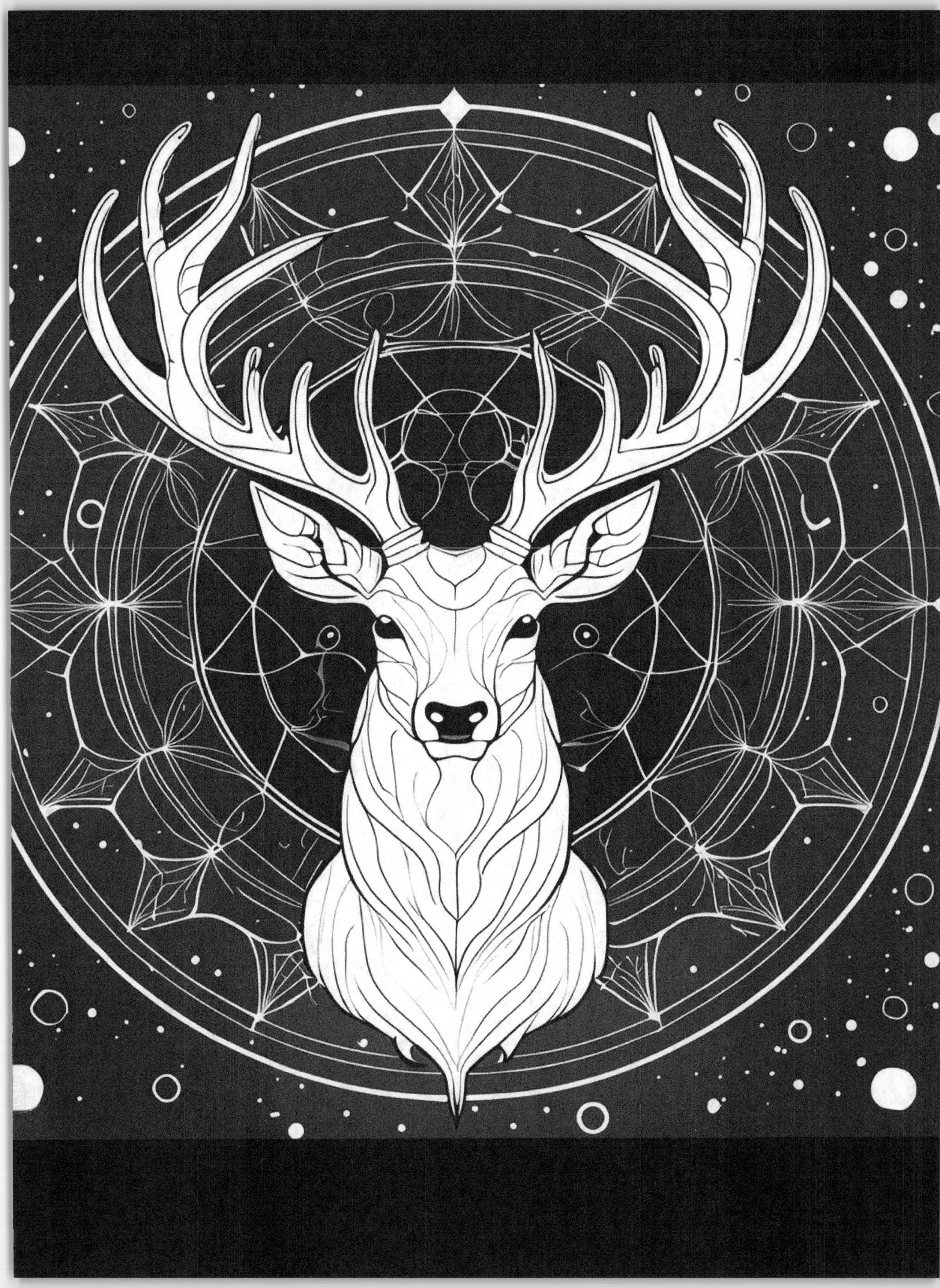

Eagle Mandala

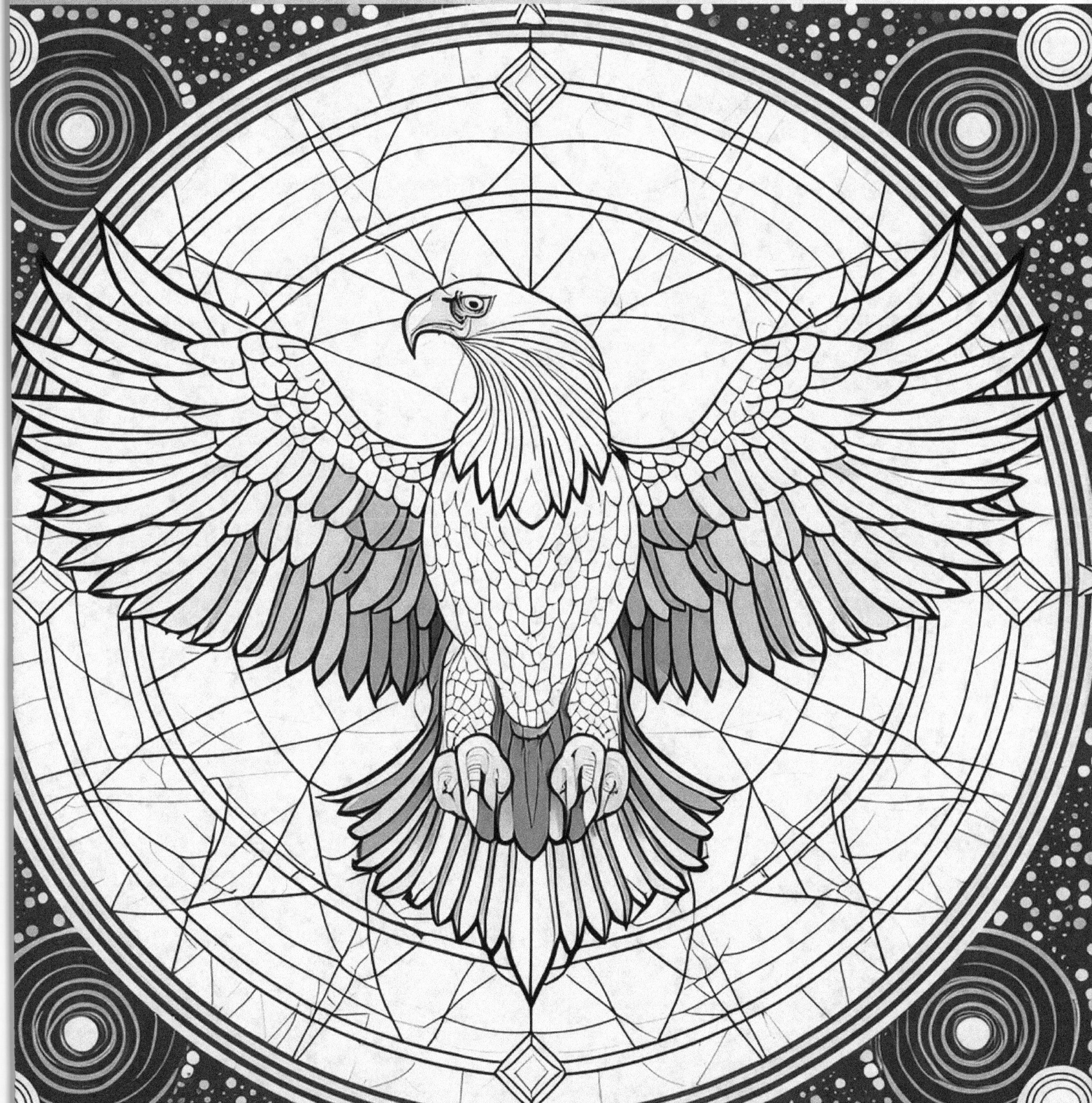

Black space rabbit Mandala

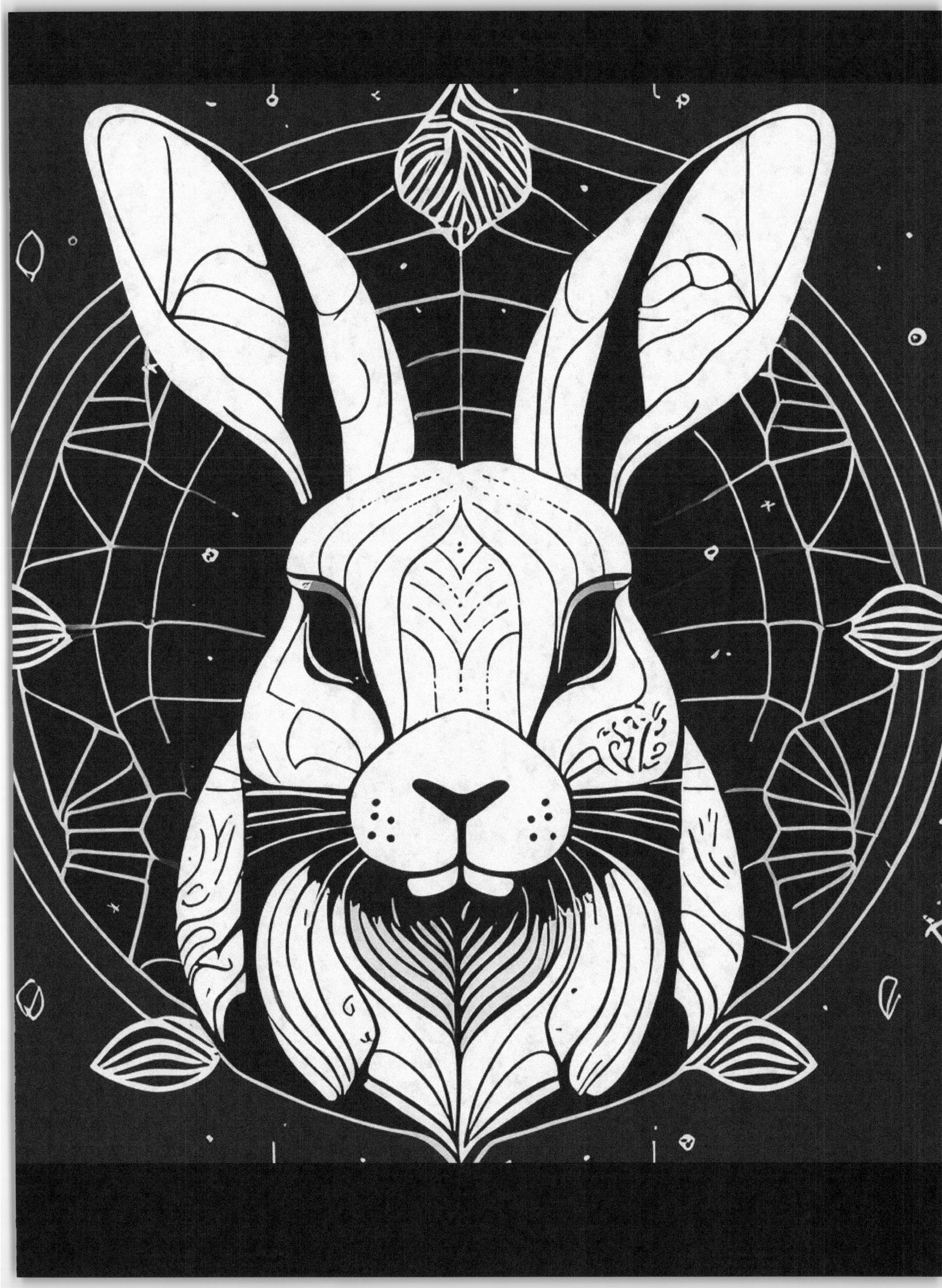

Before we part ways, I want to extend a heartfelt thank you for embarking on this colorful journey. Your dedication to improving cognition and finding joy in each stroke of color is truly inspiring. Remember, learning knows no age, and with every stroke and drawing you've empowered yourself to embrace the past, savor the present, and eagerly anticipate the future. May your mind remain sharp, your spirit vibrant, and your enthusiasm for cognitive wellness never dim. Thank you for sharing this vibrant adventure with me. As a painting tool, sketching aid, or simply to let your imagination soar, you'll have some pages at the end of the book at your disposal. Happy coloring!

www.ingramcontent.com/pod-product-compliance
Lightning Source LLC
Chambersburg PA
CBHW082210220526
45470CB00010B/3111
* 9 7 9 8 3 2 5 3 1 0 9 5 9 *